TEAM HUMAN

Douglas Feay

ACKNOWLEDGMENTS

The most important thank you belongs to God. Without God's sacrifice of His son Jesus, Team Human would be lost. Thank you to Jesus because He had the courage to follow God's plan. And a big thank you to the Holy Spirit; without Him I would probably be in jail. A very special thank you to David and Frances Matossian. Thank you to Mike, Marion, and my grandson Cameron for doing a great job editing. By the way, Cameron has never had a "B" in his life. Next comes my family, my wife Trudie, our five daughters, and many grandchildren. They all make my life worthwhile and very, very interesting. The Friday night garage guys. They really keep a guy humble. Finally, my church, a spirit-filled (24/7) place to enjoy God's presence. If you are ever in the neighborhood, come visit Sunland Neighborhood Church at 10632 Oro Vista Ave., Sunland CA 91040.

Table of Contents

Introduction

At 73 I have had a lot of Team Human members pass through my life. When I was young I did not feel compelled to share what I knew about God and the game of life. Then one day I was in a discussion with a secretary at work. She explained to me that she was a white witch. She said white witches do only good in this world. I told her that there are only two spiritual forces in this world, Jesus and Lucifer. It does not matter what type of a witch you are, good or bad, you are still part of Lucifer's team. Our discussion was interrupted by a very bad headache which she was suffering. It turned out she had had neck and head pain for the last three days. She told me that on Monday she was going to see a doctor. When Monday came, I went to see how she was doing. I was told she died Sunday while shopping at K-Mart. She had a brain aneurysm that ruptured while she was standing in line to check out. I always wished I had been more convincing about God and Lucifer during our discussion the Friday before she died.

As a member of Team Human, love now compels me to share with all Team Human members what God has done for me. What God did was keep me from dying in a very dramatic way. He has done this five times in my life that I know of. Unlike Jonah, there was no big fish, but there was a very strong voice and direct action by God when I ignored the voice. I have met other Team Human members who have had similar experiences. I have included their stories.

As a witness, love compels me to share with you what God has taught me about the game of life and what I have learned about death. You might be surprised to learn that God does not view death the same way we do.

All I can do is tell you what I have experienced in the last 72 years. But believe me when I say that the most important thing a member of Team Human can do while playing the game of life is know where you stand with Jesus. My request to God for each Team Human member is found in Ephesians 1:18: "I pray also that the eyes of your heart may be enlightened in order that you may know the hope to which he has called you."

Chapter One

My Story

Romans 8:29 from Living Letters, "For from the very beginning God decided that those who came – and all along he knew who would – should become like his son."

My relationship with God began in the primary at about age four. Bible class was held at Highland Park Presbyterian Church. I fell in love with all the Bible stories. The thought of an invisible God who has always existed and knows every thought of mine felt right to me. Then, to find out he could be your best friend, well, that was all I needed. I wanted to learn everything I could about God. In the process of learning about God, I developed a relationship with God that is almost impossible to put into words.

I was born in Monterey Park and grew up in Highland Park in East Los Angeles. I attended Annandale Elementary, Luther Burbank Junior High, and Benjamin Franklin High School. After graduating high school I attended Los Angeles City College, California State University at Los Angeles, University of California at Los Angeles, and University of California at Berkeley.

In elementary school I had a quick temper. On my second day in kindergarten I punched the teacher, Mrs. Berlotty, in the stomach. She sent me home, which was where I wanted to be in the first place. Mrs. Berlotty had a bad habit of twisting one's ear when she thought you were not paying attention, which in my case was most of the time.

The principal of Annandale was Mrs. Lincoln; she and I became very good friends. She even had a chair in her office with a brass plaque that read "Doug sits here." I occupied that wooden "chair" on average about twice a week.

I had a hard time understanding why I was the one always in trouble. It seemed as if trouble just followed me. Like the time I threw a chair at Mrs. Litton. You see, Mrs. Litton was another ear-puller. She yanked my ear when I told her why I hit Ronnie in the face after he kicked me in the butt. Ronny lived at the Optimists' Home for Boys, across the street from Annandale Elementary. As Mrs. Litton grabbed my ear and she told me not to use bad language. Well, my ear was having none of that grabbing stuff, so my ear told my arm to throw the chair. Fortunately, my arm had bad aim and the chair flew just to the right of Mrs. Litton, taking out a large glass window. That temper outburst landed me in the "chair" for about four hours.

That night I learned just how small the world is when my dad learned of my window encounter while installing a new garage door at Mrs. Litton's house that evening. My dad had a few words with the butt that had gotten kicked by Ronnie. In addition, we had to pay the school for a new window. Ronnie and I had many run-ins over the next few years. Later that year, I heard he got adopted. To this day I am a big fan of adoption. As you can see, I was a normal kid.

Attending church with me were my two brothers and my sister. I had a very normal relationship with my siblings. I was the oldest and therefore the boss.

My sister Orla was two years younger and then came my two brothers Rusty and Robert. My mother did not drive, so a few times a week she would walk to the corner market. This, of course, meant that I was left in charge of the house. However, I was the only one who understood that idea. Once, when my mom returned from the market, she noticed that Orla was nowhere to be seen. So my mom asked me where Orla was. Even though I was the one in charge, I could not remember what happened to Orla. Then it hit me. I had placed her in a dresser drawer in the bedroom. As the boss I felt that Orla needed a timeout. Of course, at four years old, she did not think she needed a timeout. Orla had fallen asleep in the dresser drawer. It was so quiet in the house I forgot where she was. My mother followed me into the bedroom, and I proceeded to open the large dresser drawer. There Orla, sound asleep on the T-shirts.

Then there was the time when my mom came home and found me in the back yard, stuffing grass into a hole in my brother Rusty's ankle. The large hole in Rusty's ankle was the result of a wooden spear. I tried to explain how the wooden spear found its way into Rusty's ankle, but Mom was just not ready to listen to me at that moment. She told me I could explain to Dad when he got home. Somehow, I could not picture Dad listening to my explanation. He was more of a hand-to-butt kind of guy.

So here is what happened. I had been watching a TV program called *Ramar of The Jungle*. The show was about a man who hunted big game in the African jungle. He always managed to save someone in distress too. Well, it had occurred to me that I could make a spear and hunt too.

However, living in East Los Angeles presented a challenge: no large jungle animals. So I drew a lion and an elephant on two large pieces of cardboard. I tied a string to each of the cardboard animals and then hung them around the necks of my two brothers. While they ran around in the backyard, I was on the roof of the garage. The roof of the garage was a great place to see the entire backyard jungle. As the animals (cardboard drawings) went by, I would throw the spear into the cardboard. The spear would stick into the ground, pulling the brother tied to the cardboard animal to the ground.

I managed to kill about two lions and one elephant before the ankle incident happened. As Rusty ran, I took careful aim and let the spear fly. Just as the spear left my hand, my foot slipped. Instead of hitting the cardboard I hit Rusty's ankle. I was amazed at how the spear went right through Rusty's ankle. When I pulled the spear from his ankle, blood started running out of a big hole. Having seen Ramar on TV use native grasses and mud to patch up a similar wound, I went to work stuffing grass into the hole in Rusty's ankle. That is about the time my mom came out the back door wanting to know what all the screaming was about.

Best Friends

Edward Saldana and Regis Braham were two close friends of mine. Regis and I shared many adventures.

Regis was one of my close friends. Regis was shorter than I, with blue eyes and blond hair, and he looked like Dennis the Menace. For those of you under 50 years old, Dennis the Menace was a cartoon character who was always in trouble.

One adventure that stands out was when we tried smoking our first cigarette. We managed to burn down Eddie Dottie's garage with his dad's new Cadillac convertible parked in it.

Regis and I were good friends, but Edward and I became like brothers. Ed and I were the same age and his mother made the best tamales I have ever eaten. I became Mrs. Saldana's son after Ed and I ate about ten tamales she was saving for dinner. During our tamale fest, Mrs. Saldana saw us eating the dinner tamales. She took a broom and started to whack us about the head and back. I learned a lot of new Spanish words that day. Once we stopped running, Ed and I heard his mother whistling for him. Whenever Mrs. Saldana wanted to call one of her children, she would whistle. Ed said he had to go back. I begged him not to go but he told me that if he ignored the whistle, it would be worse than the broom. I told Ed I would go with him. It was the least I could do since I ate half the tamales.

When we got back to the kitchen where the great tamale eat-in occurred, we got a big lecture on the right and wrong things in life. And I got my own whistle. It took me a while to learn the whistle. Ed and I got into a lot of trouble over the next few years.

Once we tied a rope to a large tree that just happened to sit next to a hairpin curve on the hillside road behind Ed's house. When a car would come around the curve one of us would swing down past the windshield of the car and drop over a guardrail, rolling down the hill. The car would screech to a halt, usually with a very angry driver yelling at the kid rolling down the hillside. We thought this was great fun.

Then it happened. It was my turn to swing and Ed was the spotter. He said, "Go" as a car came around the curve. I took off, and to my surprise the car belonged to the Los Angeles Police Department. Someone had called the police about our activities. I tried to pull up. But physics being what it is, I couldn't stop in mid-air. I pulled my feet up to avoid the windshield but managed to hit the red lights on top of the police car. After rolling down the hill I could hear the policeman yelling, "I know where you live, Doug." It was Officer John from the York Blvd. station. We became close over the next few years.

Thanks, God – Encounter One

Like all parents, God was watching out for me since I could walk. When I was three years old I climbed over our backyard fence and began exploring the world. I had gotten about a mile from home when my dad spotted me walking along Figueroa Street. Dad was on his way home from work and spotted what looked like his son walking along the street. He stopped and, sure enough, it was I. It was amazing that I had gotten almost a mile, crossing numerous side streets and many streets with traffic lights, without getting hit by a car. I only remember a large dog walking with me and how big everything looked.

My first close encounter with God that stands out in my memory came as Regis and I were walking to school. My mother did not drive, so I walked to school starting in kindergarten and ending when I graduated high school.

Regis and I were walking past a gas station when a Volkswagen made a left turn into the station. The car hit me in the left leg and bounced backwards into the street. I saw the car hit me but felt nothing. Regis looked at me and asked if I was related to Superman. I was standing there trying to figure out how an 80-pound kid could get hit by a 2,000-pound car and not get so much as a mark. While I was pondering this, the driver asked if I was ok.

I said I was fine. With that, my friend and I walked to school. By the next day I had forgotten about being hit by the car. The only time I was reminded of the car hit was when Regis would hit me with a rock to see what would happen. What happened was I got mad. I finally had to punch Regis in the nose to make him stop throwing rocks at me.

Over the next few years Ed, Regis, and I lost touch. Regis moved away and Ed joined the Navy just after high school. He received a spinal cord injury while swimming with some women at a lake in Italy. He lived another twenty years as quadriplegic.

When God Speaks – Encounter Two

During my life God has spoken to me in several different ways. The first and most prevalent way God talks to me is through the Bible. I believe this is the way most of us hear God. A second way God has spoken to me is through prayer. When God has answered one of my prayers, I know He is listening. There is a third way, which few people get to experience: His voice. Like Jonah, God gave me instructions and I did not follow them. God can speak to us directly if He chooses to do so. Jonah 1:1, "The word of the Lord came to Jonah son of Amittal: Go to the great city of Nineveh and preach against it, because its wickedness has come up before me…"

I was nineteen years old and in college when God intervened again. Unlike the Volkswagen incident, this time God spoke to me. I was driving in my 1955 hot rod Chevy looking for someone to race. I had rebuilt my '55 Chevy into a very fast car and loved street racing. So while I was stopped at a red light, a red MG pulled up next to me. The stoplight was at the corner of Los Feliz Boulevard and Central Avenue in Glendale, California. I looked over at the MG and revved the car engine a few times to get the driver's attention. The driver looked at me with that "I could beat your Chevy" look. So the challenge was given.

But before the light turned green, God spoke to me and said, "Don't move." The voice I heard was a deep-sounding voice. Of course, I did what all Team Human members have done through the years and ignored His voice. I acted like I did not hear God.

When you choose to ignore God speaking either through the Bible or directly, you need to be prepared for the consequences. God always gets what He wants. In the case of the Jewish nation, they ignored God and had to spend 40 years wandering in the desert before they could enter into the Promised Land.

Fortunately for me, God did not decide to let me wander around Glendale, but He did paralyze me. As the red light turned green, I went for the gas pedal. At the same time, God paralyzed my legs. Nothing would work from my waist down. I looked over at the driver of the MG and just shrugged my shoulders.

The person behind me honked his horn but when God is doing his thing, there is nothing you can do. So next time you're behind a car that's not moving, don't honk. They might be doing something with God.

While I was sitting there thinking about why God was not letting me race, something happened. When God takes action, the word _but_ almost always comes into play. The word _but_ is then followed by something happening. "But, Lord," I asked, "why did you paralyze me?"

His answer to my question came in the form of a very big and fast black car running the red light. While I had a green light, from the left of the intersection came a fast-moving black car that ran his red light. Had I gotten to the gas pedal and raced into the intersection, my 1955 Chevy would have been t-boned. There is no way I could have lived through that accident. The black car was going about 50 miles an hour. No Chevy ever built could survive being t-boned at 50 miles an hour. My car would have been smashed into three or four large pieces of scrap metal.

As soon as the large black car had passed through the intersection, my legs started working. My mind, on the other hand, was not yet ready to continue with life. The red MG and I moved through the intersection very slowly. We moved on down the road a ways, and I pulled over to the first parking space I could find to try and figure out what just happened. I am sure the guy in the red MG was wondering why I did not race him when the light turned green, but I know he was very happy I did not race him.

God's Peace – Encounter Three

The best way to describe my next encounter with God is to quote from Philippians, Chapter Four, verses 6 and 7. This translation is from Living Letters. "Don't worry about anything; instead, pray about everything; tell God your needs and don't forget to thank him for his answers. If you do this you will experience God's peace, which is far more wonderful than human mind can understand. His peace will keep your thoughts and your hearts quiet and at rest as you trust in Christ Jesus."

This encounter with God came in a very unique way. I had just closed Sears and was on my way home. It was about 2:00 am. I was driving home on Colorado Boulevard when I stopped for a red light. You notice how God seems to wait until I am stopped at a red traffic light before He takes action?

So there I am, it is 2:00 am, and I am waiting for the light to change. I would have never in my wildest dreams thought God would visit me at 2:00 am, stopped at a red light on Colorado Boulevard, but He did. It is interesting to note that while waiting for the light to change, my mind was definitely not on God. I was driving my beloved '55 Chevy and thinking about a very pretty girl I had just met that day at work. Plus, I had a midterm exam in a few days, which I had not studied for. However, God is going to do what God is going to do in spite of our current condition.

What God did was to sit down next to me in my '55

Chevy. I felt a person sit next to me and give me a hug. Now, having experienced God speaking to me, I was not taken back by having an invisible person next to me. How did I know the person next to me was invisible? I looked. Summoning up a little courage, I glanced over my shoulder and, guess what, there was nobody where there should have been somebody.

About the time I began to question what was going on, another strange event occurred. Now I have had many hugs in my life. But this hug, well, let's just say it was out of this world. Or more accurately, I was pulled out of this world. Thoughts started leaving me like rats from a sinking ship. My brain soon began to empty of all thoughts and wants. If you would have asked me for the keys to my beloved '55 Chevy, I would have gladly given them to you. I was slowly losing all interest in this world. It was as if I was not part of it, nor did I feel any belonging to this world. I was overtaken by a peace that I had never experienced and have not experienced since then.

Looking back on that event, I have tried to imagine when in a person's life you would expect to have that kind of peace. The only time I can think of when you could expect that kind of peace is when you die. I can't tell you how long I was sitting at that red light. I do remember four light changes. So I guess that would be about three or four minutes. It felt a lot longer than just a few minutes.

So now the question is why God was doing this. I can understand why the Volkswagen and intersection event happened. It was to protect me and keep me from dying. But this event has me scratching my head. It has been about 50 years since my out-of-this-world experience, and I still have not figured out why. So I have decided to just accept it and not think about why. In fact, over the years I have decided not to question what God has done for me, just accept it and not think about why.

Vietnam – Encounter Four

The next time God saved my life was in Vietnam while I was being shot at by a sniper. I was stationed in Vietnam in 1970. I had a cousin who had been in country for about six years. We both ended up at Cam Ranh Bay. It was about a four-mile walk to see him.

Because my duty was 12 noon to 12 midnights, I always ended up walking to see him about 3:00 am. Walking along at night on a lonely road between the sea and jungle would not have been that bad if it were not for the sniper. There was a local sniper who was hidden somewhere along the road I had to walk on to visit my cousin Denny.

My first encounter with the sniper was on my first trip back to the 6th Convalescent Center (6th C.C.) north of my cousin's location. I was somewhere near an empty French-style building when the bullets started to fly. It was late and I was about halfway back when I heard what sounded like rounds whizzing next to my head. Bullets make a very unforgettable sound when they pass within a few inches of your ear.

Anyway, once my brain notified my feet that we were being shot at, my feet made a dash for the beach just east of the road. I was surprised but glad the sniper was such a bad shot. I figured he was a local guy who would shoot at GIs occasionally and was not the greatest of shots. Or, on the other hand, he was a very good shot and God decided it was not my time to go.

Whatever the reason, I was determined not to let the sniper keep me from seeing my cousin. Over the next several weeks I would stealthily pass the area by moving in and around bushes, on the beach, or whatever I could find. Sometimes while walking I would forget about the sniper, but he would remind me.

Our little duels, me running, him shooting, went on for many weeks. On one occasion, I got a little cocky. I stood on the road and did jumping jacks, hoping the strange sight would confuse him. It must have worked because he stopped shooting for about five minutes. Then I ran.

I guess I was not the only one he shot at. He must have shot at someone important because at about 4:00 am on my last trip to see my cousin, an attack helicopter came from over the ocean and used his Gatling gun to take out the hill where the sniper was. It was a very strange thing to see. The Gatling gun fires about 6,000 rounds a minute. When the helicopter put his tail up and his nose down and fired, it looked as if a red laser was firing at the hill. It was an amazing display of light and power, and I had a front row seat. In fact, I was the only person in the theater, except for the poor sniper. I never had the chance to go down that road again to see if the sniper had been replaced.

One thing that has always haunted me was: why me? When God saved my life, several times, God never felt the need to explain why me. Don't misunderstand me, I am very grateful to be alive, but when you know that you have been singled out for something special, it seems to be Team Human nature to want to know why. It is like when you're sitting in class and the teacher says to the class that you are her favorite student and she has a special gift for you. You know that you did not deserve that special gift, but the teacher did pick you, and you wonder why me? The kid next to you is just as deserving of the special gift as you are, but the teacher chose you.

When I look at all the people that I feel should have had their lives extended, I feel very guilty for being given the gift of life several times.

0.1 Percent Chance of Life – Encounter Five

You would think that after having God save my life at least four times I would be used to it. Not really. With God, everything is an adventure.

So there I am, watching the Raiders on TV while eating a sandwich at my youngest daughter's birthday party in Temecula. Suddenly—that seems to be the way God always saves my life—I felt something inside my body break. Then I started sweating. The kind of dripping-wet sweat you would get after an hour or two's workout. Mine occurred in about three minutes. I went and found a bed to lie down on.

My wife noticed I was not watching the TV and found me lying on a bed in a pool of sweat. She asked me if I was ok. I told her to call an ambulance. I thought I might have an aortic artery leaking.

Three weeks later, I woke up in the ICU ward at the U.C.L.A. medical center. I was told that my pancreas had exploded, and they had to remove it along with my large intestine, leaving me a 0.1 percent chance of living until the next day. It seems that I was in organ failure and had four different types of bacteria, along with candida albicans, growing in my blood. The doctor was sure I was not going to live through the night. Kimberly, my wife's lifetime friend, told her she should get a funeral dress.

Of course, the doctor had not asked God about whether or not it was my time to go home, to Heaven, that is. Well, here I am, years later and writing this book.

It took about two years before I could walk. It turns out that when you spend a month in a coma and a year in bed, your muscles shrink. Who knew? Now, to get back what has shrunken takes three or four times as long as it did to shrink. Thanks to my wife, who knew very little about caring for a bedridden person and is now an expert, I am back to normal. Well, my normal anyway.

Of course, there is a lot more to the story. If you want to find out more, you can find my story on Caringbridge. com. My wonderful daughter is documenting my journey by writing about me on that website.

Chapter Two

Harm, Ryan, and Demon

One thing I am always looking for is someone who has had experiences with God similar to mine. It is always nice to know you're not the only one. I have met only three people who have had God speak to them. Two of them have only heard God's voice once. Those two people's names are Harm and Ryan. The reason God spoke to us was to save our lives. The third person I know who has heard God's voice and actually receives instructions from God is a self-appointed minister named Demon.

Harm

I met Harm at a family camp where he was the speaker. Harm was the pastor of a very large church and the president of a small Christian college back East. Harm and I were talking after dinner one night, and I asked him if God had ever spoken to him directly. To my surprise, he said, "Yes, once." When Harm was a teenager, he used to ice-fish with his uncle. Ice fishing is done by cutting a hole in the frozen lake, dropping a fishing line into the hole, and waiting. If you're going to ice-fish all night, you need a small icehouse that is pushed onto the ice over the fish hole. One night while Harm and his uncle were fishing, God spoke to Harm. God told Harm to go outside.

This seemed like an unreasonable thing to do since it was about 15 degrees below zero and the wind was blowing. It is very interesting that when God talks to us, He tends to ask us to do unreasonable things. Team Human members always seem to respond to God the same way: by saying no. You would think that with all of the interaction God has had with Team Human over the last 5,000-plus years, we would respond to God's orders in a positive way.

Harm said no to God's request to go outside. Remember I said God is a God of action? In Jonah's case God had a large fish swallow him. With Harm God was also very dramatic. Suddenly, Harm's body stood up and started walking. Harm was not in control of his body anymore. God was. When God decides to take control, there is nothing you can do but enjoy it. So out into the freezing night went Harm's body, and of course his mind went too.

When he was about twenty feet from the icehouse, Harm's uncle leaned out of the door and began to shout at Harm. Harm could not hear what his uncle was saying. However, what happened in the next few seconds saved Harm and his uncle from sure death.

As Harm's uncle was leaning out of the icehouse, it blew up. A huge ball of fire roared over Harm's uncle and threw him to the ice, pushing him out the door and across the ice. It turned out that the propane tank was leaking gas. The propane tank was right next to Harm, and the explosion would have killed him and his uncle.

Ryan

I met Ryan a few years ago while in the hospital recovering from the demise of my pancreas. Ryan was our pastor and was visiting me. I asked Ryan if he had ever heard God's voice. He had.

Ryan was hiking when God told him to go back down the trail. The idea of going back down the trail when it had taken so much time and energy to get where he was just seemed wrong to Ryan. So Ryan told God no, just as Harm did. So God took action.

As Ryan walked up the trail, his feet began to gain weight. With every step, his feet got heavier until he could no longer move them. It is interesting to see how God deals with each of us differently. In Harm's case, God took over his body and made him walk out into the icy storm. With Ryan, He let him go on until he could no longer physically continue. I have met Christians who continue on when God said not to. Guess what? They get so bogged down, they cannot continue and end up going backwards.

Ryan turned around and started back down the trail. As he walked, his feet got lighter. Then it happened. The spot where Ryan had been walking was suddenly hit by a rockslide. Ryan would have been killed.

Demon

Without a doubt, Demon is one of the most unique people I have ever met. While attending college, I and seven other students went to Guatemala during the summer months in 1965 as missionaries. Our group stayed at a Christian camp at Lake Atitlan. Our job was to build a foundation for a building that was to be used by about 300 people. The camp had a cook named Demon. He cooked the best-tasting food I had ever eaten. Demon was married and had eighteen children. Demon and I developed a friendship due the fact that I was the only one in camp who could fix cars. Demon had a 1952 Ford panel truck that needed to run in order to pick up 500 tortillas that a woman in town made. She was paid about three dollars for 500 tortillas. That seemed to me to be a little underpaid for a lot of work, but I found out that the average wage for a day's work was about 50 cents.

The Ford panel truck had a flathead six-cylinder that needed a lot of care. I got the truck running and, during my stay at the camp, spent time with Demon. During one of our conversations I asked Demon if he had ever heard God speak to him. He told me that he would spend about three days out of every month talking to God. This surprised me. I was familiar with praying to God and I had been given instructions by God, but I had never carried on a conversation or received instruction from God on a regular basis. My skeptical nature prompted me to test Demon. I had received a letter saying that my blood brother Ed had been sick. Ed and I became blood brothers after watching the blood brother ceremony on TV. We stuck our fingers with a pocketknife and put our bleeding fingers together to become blood brothers. I think we were about ten years old when we did the blood brother thing. So I had told Demon to pray for Ed because Ed was sick, but I did not know how sick he was or even what was wrong with him. I never told Demon that Ed was quadriplegic either. About two weeks had gone by when Demon told me he had talked to God and this is what God told him. God had told Demon that Ed had broken his leg after running into a wall while racing his wheelchair down a hospital corridor. God informed Demon that surgery was done to repair Ed's leg. During surgery, Ed's heart stopped, and the surgeon had to do CPR. God also told Demon that He was not going to take Ed home to Heaven yet. Demon also told me that at the time of Ed's accident, he was wearing black pants and a red shirt. I was amazed at the detail and amount of information Demon had about Ed and his illness. I was also not sure of everything Demon told me. I had no way to check what Demon said to me until I got home. When I got home, the very first thing I did was to walk up the street to Ed's house and find out what happened while I was gone. When I got to Ed's house I told Ed that he had a broken leg while racing his wheelchair and that his heart stopped during surgery. I even said he was wearing black pants and a red shirt. Ed's mouth hung open and his eyes got very big as he asked me how I found out about his broken leg. And, yes, he had on black pants and a red shirt at the time of the accident. So I told him about Demon.

Years later, I met up with one of the missionaries I worked with in Guatemala. The subject of Demon came up and he told me a story about what had happened between Demon and him. He said that one day, Demon informed him that he was going to a small town in southern Mexico. Demon told the missionary that God wanted him to go there but did not say why. The trip would take several weeks and cover over 1,500 miles of roads so bad that a four-wheel-drive truck would have trouble. Demon was driving a 1952 Ford panel truck. Demon was going to take five or six of his children with him, but his wife would take over cooking for the camp while he was gone. While we are on the subject of cooking, I once asked Demon where he learned to cook. His French toast was the best-tasting toast I ever ate. Demon also baked bread for the camp. In a typical Demon-like answer, he looked me in the eye and said he had never learned how to cook. He said he needed a job when he heard the camp needed a cook, so he applied and got the job because God told him to. Ok, I said, but what about not knowing how to cook? "Well," he told me, "take the bread I cook for an example. I mix a little flour and water together, put it in the oven, and say a prayer." I asked him if he had ever heard of yeast and letting the bread rise before baking. Demon looked at me with that look that says, "I have not a clue about what you a talking about." Demon said that when God tells him to do something, he does it and it is God's job to take care of the details. So back to our impossible trip to southern Mexico. The missionary argued against the trip and told Demon it was a very bad idea. So Demon thanked the missionary for his advice and went to Mexico. Demon traveled 1,500 miles and stayed one night in a small town. While there, he talked with a lady about her life and she became a Christian. It just so happened that she had four tires and a battery that fit Demon's 1952 Ford panel truck. The next day Demon left for home. Five years after Demon had gone to Mexico, the missionaries at our camp found out the lady that Demon had led to Christ had started an orphanage, hospital, and school.

The last time Demon and I talked, he said God had asked him to go to Guatemala City and help take care of the hundreds of orphaned children that lived on the streets.

Chapter Three

Communications, God's Style

Communicating is the most important aspect of playing the game of life. I became very aware of how important communication is while in the army. In the army, I had two bosses: the colonel in charge of the morgue and a lieutenant in charge of the company I was assigned to. Since I lived in married housing and not the company housing, I only reported to the company maybe once or twice a year while reporting to the colonel every day. I had put in for a three-week leave to visit my relatives in Idaho. It took me a month to train a replacement for the morgue. Once I had a replacement, the colonel signed my orders for the leave. The vacation orders were submitted to Personnel, and in about two weeks I signed out of the company and drove 1,500 miles to Twin Falls, Idaho. About a week into my vacation I got a call from my friend Mike. Mike had a doctorate in psychology. He was a corporal, in charge of testing patients recovering from long-term hospital stays. Mike did not have much use for the army. He even painted his office pink to upset the sergeant who was his boss. So, Mike called me and said I was listed by the company as being AWOL, absent without leave. AWOL can be punishable by few years in the pokey. I called the company and was told the lieutenant had not signed my leave orders. I said my colonel had signed the orders. Well, it turned out that two signatures were required for leave. Personnel had not bothered to inform me that two signatures were needed for my leave when the orders were turned in by the colonel. The colonel said he was not aware of that rule. I guess no one who worked in the morgue had ever gone on vacation. I cut my vacation short and drove with my two-year-old daughter and very upset wife the 1,500 miles back to Letterman General Hospital. I informed the lieutenant that I was not impressed with the army's ability to communicate with its soldiers. I was told that a correction to the morning report would fix the situation. Of course, that could have been told to me over the phone before I drove the 1,500 miles back to the company.

As you read earlier, God has communicated with me by voice, actions, and of course through the Bible. I have yet to get any instructions via dreams. I must admit that God's communications with voice and actions were most dramatic. However, the most prevalent way of communications from God is through the Bible. All the information ever needed to play the game of life is written there. Yet for Team Human members who do not have a relationship with God, the Bible may be difficult to understand. It seems they would put more trust in a book written by a scientist than God. So for those of you who need scientific verification of the Bible, here it is.

I am going to use what is called the Scientific Method. The scientific method uses an idea or theorem then proceeds to prove that idea via scientific experiment (observations and data) taken from the physical universe. In addition to scientific verification, the theorem needs to be able to predict what might happen or be discovered in the future. For the theorems of our study I am going to use 4,000- to 6,000-year-old physical cosmological models from several cultures and religions, then evaluate those physical cosmological models against the current physical cosmology model which has been developed from current scientific observations and data. Reason dictates that a 4,000- to 6,000-year-old physical cosmological model should not correspond with a model based on current scientific knowledge.

Theorems

Hindu Model

The Brahmanda Universe from the Hindu Rigveda describes an oscillating universe starting from a single point called the Bindu. From this single point everything in the universe, including all gods, was created. This cosmic egg collapses and expands infinitely.

Chinese Model

Pangu was born inside of an egg which was split apart. The upper half became the sky and the lower the earth. After about 18,000 years Pangu died and his body formed the earth and humans. The Chinese viewed China as the center of the earth, which was a square. The sky was split into four areas centered around the pole star. The sun and moon were gods.

Egyptian Model

Ra, the sun god, was born out of primal oceans of chaos. This state of chaos was called Nun. The primal oceans contained all that was needed for creation. Ra used his will to emerge from the chaotic state to give birth to gods and goddesses. Egyptians considered the earth the foundation of the universe, and the earth was rectangular in shape.

Mesopotamian Model

The Mesopotamian civilizations of Judea, Canaan, Babylon, and Sumer all had the same line of thinking when it came to the concept of the cosmos. Using water as a primordial element, they described the earth as a ship floating on "waters of the deep." Above the earth was a solid dome covered with water which would rain down on the earth. The origins of the deities were the stars. Deities were the creators of all life and physical matter.

Jewish Model (Torah)

Of all the early models of Creation only the Torah presents very specific steps in a very specific order for Creation. The Creation story is found in book one of the

Torah, called Genesis, and was written by Moses. The following is the order from Genesis (Bereishit):

1) Chapter 1:3, God said, "Let there be light, and there was light."

2) Chapter 1:4, God saw the light that it was good, and God separated between the light and between the darkness.

3) Chapter 1:6, God said, "Let there be an expanse in the midst of the water, and let it be a separation between water and water."

4) Chapter 1:7, And God made the expanse and it separated between the water that was below the expanse and the water that was above the expanse…

5) Chapter 1:9, God said, "Let the water that is beneath the heavens gather into one place, and let the dry land appear…"

6) Chapter 1:11, God said, "Let the earth sprout vegetation, seed yielding herbs and fruit trees producing fruit according to its kind in which its seed is found…"

7) Chapter 1:14, And God said, "Let there be luminaries in the expanse of the heavens, to separate between the day and between the night, and they shall be for signs and for appointed seasons and for days and years."

8) Chapter 1:20, And God said, "Let the waters swarm a swarming of living creatures, and let fowl fly over the earth, across the expanse of the heavens."

9) Chapter 1:24, And God said, "Let the earth bring forth living creatures according to their kind, cattle and creeping things and the beasts of the earth according to their kind," and it was so.

10) Chapter 1:26, And God said, "Let us make man in our image, after our likeness, and they shall rule over the fish of the sea and over the fowl of the heavens and over the animals and over all the earth and over all the creeping things that creep upon the earth."

Current Physical Cosmology

Before we compare the current physical cosmology model with the models above, we need to have a brief look at how the data is chronicled. Science uses the twenty-four-hour system. So if you are looking at data that indicates how old something is, you can get time intervals on the order of tens of thousands of years. However, there are Christians who interpret the creation period in Genesis as literally a twenty-four-hour creation day. Looking into the history of the church with respect to the twenty-four-hour creation day versus the seven days of creation, I was surprised to discover that the debate can be traced back to about AD 37. AD 37 is about as old as you can get when it comes to the church's roots. I found a very good website that has an extremely accurate and timely discussion of the history of the creation day debate. The website was created by and is maintained by Robert I. Bradshaw. Hundreds of hours of work and diligent research went into this website, and the information it contains is very helpful in understanding how the early church interpreted the length of the twenty-four-hour creation day. Most of the historical information contained in this study came from that website. In the developing early Christian church, opponents to the church alleged that Christianity was a new religion and not to be taken seriously. The early church writers' answer to this charge was that in reality, Christianity was the oldest religion, continuing God's work with the Jews, and therefore the truest religion. To prove their claim, the early church writers used the creation story in Genesis. The table below (Bradshaw) shows how some early church writers viewed the length of the Days of Creation.

As you can see from Table 1 there was great disagreement about the length of the creation day. Before the year 300 AD, only about 10 percent of the early church writers believed in a figurative (longer than) twenty-four-hour creation day. After the year 300 AD, about 55 percent of the early church writers believed in a figurative (longer than) twenty-four-hour creation day.

TABLE 1

Date	Writer	24-Hour	Figurative	Unclear	Reference
c. 20-c. AD 50	Philo		X		*Creation* 13
AD 37/38 c100	Josephus			X	*Antiquities* 1.1.1 (27-33)
c. 100-c. 165	Justin Martyr			X	
110-18-	Tatian			X	
c. 180	Theophilus of Antioch	X			*Autolycus* 2.11-12
c. 115-202	Irenaeus of Lyons			X	
c. 150 0c. 215	Clement of Alexandria		X		*Miscellanies* 6.16
c. 160-c. 225	Tertullian			X	
c. 160-240	Julius Africanus			X	

TABLE 1

Date	Writer	24-Hour	Figurative	Unclear	Reference
170-236	Hippolytus of Rome			X	*Genesis*, 1.5
185-253	Origen		X		*Celsus*. 6.50,60
d. 311	Methodius	X			*Chastity* 5.7
240-320	Lactantius	X			*Institutes* 7.14
d. c. 304	Victorinus of Pettau	X			*Creation*
263-339	Eusebius of Caesarea			X	
306-373	Ephrem the Surian	X			*Commentary on Genesis* 1.1
315-404	Epiphanius of Salamis	X			*Panarion*, 1.1.1
329-379	Basil of Caesarea	X			*Hexameron*, 2.8

TABLE 1

Date	Writer	24-Hour	Figurative	Unclear	Reference
330-394	Gregory of Nyssa			X	
330-390	Gregory of Nazianxus			X	
d. 387	Cyril of Jerusalem	X			*Catechetical Lectures* 12.5
339-397	Ambrose of Milan	X			*Hexameron*, 1.10.3-7
374-407	John Chrysostom			X	
347-419/420	Jerome			X	
354-430	Augustine of Hippo		X		*Literal*, 4.22.39

Table 2 shows some of the early church writers who believed the creation day was at least 1,000 years long or more, based on the scriptures in Genesis 1, Psalms 90:4, 2 Peter 3:8, and the biblical genealogy.

As you have read above, the debate about time goes back to the roots of Christianity. I have come to the con-

TABLE 2			
Clement of Alexandria	c. 150- c. 215	5,592	*Miscellanies* 1.21
Julius Africanus	c.160-240	5,500	*Chronology*, Fragment 1
Hippolytus of Rome	170-236	5,500	*Daniel*, 4
Origen	185-253	< 10,000	*Celsus*, 1.20
Eusebius of Caesarea	263-339	5,228	*Chronicle*
Augustine of Hippo	354-430	< 5,600	*City* 12.11

clusion that the debate about time is not as important as the debate about who created the universe. Team members who do not know God need to understand that the only way we got here is through the creation of all by God. It is time for Christians to set aside the debate about time and join the debate about who did the creating. For the rest of this scientific method I will be using the order of creation as known through today's science. For any references to time I will be using what today's science uses, the twenty-four-hour time system.

Scientific Data

Big Bang

In 1927 Georges Lemaître proposed an expanding model for the universe to explain the observed redshifts of spiral nebulae. He based his theory on the work of Einstein and De Sitter and Friedmann's equations for an expanding universe.

In 1931, Lemaître proposed in his hypothesis of the primeval atom that the universe began with the "explosion" of the "primeval atom" (Big Bang).

The accidental discovery of cosmic microwave background radiation in 1964 is a major development in modern physical cosmology. It was discovered accidentally by American radio astronomers Arno Penzias and Robert Woodrow Wilson as they experimented with the Holmdel Horn Antenna. The discovery was important evidence for a hot early universe (Big Bang).

The Big Bang is now the accepted and documented beginning of creation.

Currently no scientific data exist concerning the "primeval atom." In his book *The Trouble with Physics*, Dr. Lee Smolin suggests that since no evidence exists for strings after 70 years of looking, they just do not exist. One could conclude that before the Big Bang, nothing existed.

The Torah's Chapter 1:3 from the previous listed models is the only one that agrees with today's cosmic data about the being of creation for the physical universe.

Our Galaxy and Earth

Around 8 billion years ago, the Milky Way began forming. Between 5 and 4 billion years ago, the sun and planets began their formation. About 4.5 billion years ago, the sun is formed and goes through a series of changes until it matures.

About 4.4 billion years ago, the oceans began forming. Earth's oceans contain two types of water. Light water (normal water) and heavy water. A normal water molecule is made of two hydrogen atoms and one oxygen atom. In heavy water, a normal hydrogen atom is replaced with deuterium, which is like hydrogen except that it has an extra neutron in its nucleus. Out of every 10,000 water molecules on Earth, three are heavy water molecules. Science has discovered through the European Space Agency's (ESA) Rosetta spacecraft that space has about three or more times the ratio of heavy water molecules than earth's water. If earth's oceans had the same ratio of heavy water as space, life on earth would not have occurred. Sometime before the formation of the oceans, light and heavy water were formed and then separated.

Examining the previous listed models, we see the Torah Chapter 1:4,6,7 agrees with today's science. These three verses can be interpreted as 1) earth's early sun would have looked opaque through a very thick atmosphere, 2) formation of a stable water cycle, and 3) light water forming in space and on earth.

Oceans and Land

After light water was separated from heavy, the oceans were formed with light water being the predominate form. The process which caused the oceans to fill with light water is not known. What is known is that life began in the oceans. Very primitive single-celled plant life formed between 4.3 billion and 3.5 billion years ago. During this time land began forming. The earliest known rock is about 4.1 billion years old. Chapter 1:9 of the Torah talks about the formation of the oceans and land. None of the other creation stories talk about this process.

Atmosphere

Scientists believe that for half of Earth's 4.6-billion-year history, the atmosphere contained almost no oxygen. Cyanobacteria, or blue-green algae, became the first microbes to produce oxygen by photosynthesis, as long ago as 3.5 billion years ago. About 850–540 million years ago (0.85–0.54 billion years ago), atmospheric oxygen levels increased from 15 percent to over 30 percent as continents broke apart and reassembled, resulting in violent climate changes. As the oxygen increased, the atmosphere went from a cloudy fog to a clear atmosphere much like today's atmosphere. As the atmosphere cleared, the sun and moon could be seen, and they had a much greater effect on living organisms.

Chapter 1, verses 11 and 14 of the Torah can be interpreted as describing the beginnings of plants on earth and the final transformation of the atmosphere from translucent to transparent. None of the other creation stories mention this.

Sea Life

About 730 million years ago, multicellular life forms inhabited the oceans. 530 million years ago, the true vertebrates appeared. This was also the time that the trilobites appear. Trilobites would be around for about 200 million years. The Torah, Chapter 1, verse 20, gives us the process that produced all big and small sea creatures along with all birds. None of the other creation stories talk about this.

Land Life

Plants and arthropods began moving to land about 450 million years age. The lungfish appears about 417 million years ago and has the ability to breathe air and survive on land. For the next 445 million-plus years, life continues to expand both in the sea and on land. In Chapter 1, verse 24 of the Torah God gives us the land process which created all land creatures.

Genus Homo

At around 2.2 million years ago, humans appear on land. Humans present a very unique and exceptional form of life on the planet. Before the appearance of humans all life forms existed within the influences of physical and biological realms. With the introduction of humans a third realm of influence on life begins, the spiritual. Humans possess a soul.

Science has never been able to find any scientific historical data on how man was created. Science has millions of years of data on all the other living creatures on earth. Man has only been here about 2 million years. Two million years is not enough time for any of the known processes to have produced man. That means that either God produced man or aliens from some unknown worlds produced man. Chapter 1, verse 26 of the Torah says that God made man. The Torah and science have agreed on all the historical scientific creation data up to this point. Up to this point God has commanded creation to happen. That means that there are processes that would leave a historic scientific trail that can be followed. But how do you find any historic data when there are no processes that were used to create man. God says that He used hands to make man. Using hands to create man from dirt, in my opinion, would not leave any historic data to find.

I am going with the Torah and say that God created man.

None of the other creation stories say that God created man.

TABLE 3		Hindu Model	Chinese Model	Egypt Model	Meso. Model	Jewish Model
Current order						
Big Bang		No	No	No	No	Yes
Galaxy & Earth		No	No	No	No	Yes
Oceans & Land		No	No	No	No	Yes
Atmosphere		No	No	No	No	Yes
Sea Life		No	No	No	No	Yes
Land Life		No	No	No	No	Yes
Genus Homo		No	No	No	No	Yes

Conclusion

Looking at Table 3, it is apparent that the 4,000-year-old Genesis account of creation is the only document that has the same order of creation as currently known to science. I would challenge anyone to find a 4000-year-old document that has an order of creation that matches what science has discovered.

Moses was the author of Genesis. He had the highest education possible for his time. Similarly, all the other documents used in the comparison were written by learned men. Yet not one document, except for Genesis, can by verified via comparison to science. It would have been impossible for Moses to write down the correct order of creation with the level of knowledge that existed during Moses' lifetime. The only way Moses could have obtained that knowledge would be from God. The Bible has thousands of scientific and historical facts that are verifiable using today's knowledge. Of all the books in Team Human's library, the Bible is the only one authored by God.

Predictions

Prediction One

In order for our theorem to have validity, it should be able to predict future events or conditions. So what can Genesis tell us about what Team Human may discover in the future?

God said, "Let the waters swarm a swarming of living creatures, and let fowl fly over the earth, across the expanse of the heavens." This would be the production of all big and small sea creatures and of all birds. The fact that God told the waters to produce life means that there is a process that God used in creating life. That same process would be working today on any planet that has the same conditions as earth.

On 28 September 1969 near the town of Murchison, Victoria, in Australia, a meteorite separated into three fragments. Fragments were found over an area larger than 8 square miles, with individual mass up to 15 lb. One piece weighing 1.3 lb. fell through a roof and into a haystack. The Murchison meteorite contains common amino acids such as glycine, alanine, and glutamic acid as well as unusual ones like isovaline and pseudoleucine. A complex mixture of alkanes was isolated as well. A specific family of amino acids called diamino acids was identified in the Murchison meteorite as well. A 2010 study identified 14,000 molecular compounds including 70 amino acids in a sample of the meteorite. The limited scope of the analysis provides for a potential 50,000 or more unique molecular compositions with the possibility of millions of distinct organic compounds in the meteorite.

It is apparent that life exists outside of earth. So it is not unusual to expect life on planets similar to Earth.

Predictions Two and Three

And God said, "Let us make man in our image, after our

likeness, and they shall rule over the fish of the sea and over the fowl of the heavens and over the animals and over all the creeping things that creep upon the earth." This is the creation of mankind.

When God created man, He did so outside of the process He set up for plants and animals. The statement "let us make man in our own image" definitely places man outside of the plant and animal creation process. When you look at the fossil record, it becomes apparent that evolution is a big part of the life cycle of plants and animals. Their evolutionary process took almost 750 million years. Yet man has been on the planet for only about 2 million years.

There are many articles written about the high mathematical odds against evolution producing human life in only 2 million years. However, I have read very little on the mathematical odds of evolution producing a soul or spiritual aspect of life. Team Human members are the only creatures on this planet with a soul or spiritual connection to God. When God said, "Let us make man in our likeness," God was including in that likeness a soul. A soul puts man on a communication plan with God that is not available to plants and animals. Whatever system God used to create man is unique to this planet and confined to this planet. It is apparent to me that: 1) there will never be an evolutionary link between man and animals, and 2) the only life we will find on other planets will be plants and animals but no life with a soul.

Chapter Four

Game of Life

It is 2:30 in the morning in the middle of the Mojave Desert and I am with a fellow geologist named Rich. Rich and I are discussing life. About an hour into our talk we got around to discussing existence of the soul. Rich's view is simple. You're born and you live and you die, turning into a pile of dust, no soul. No matter what I said, Rich would not acknowledge the existence of the soul. I had a very hard time understanding his viewpoint. I had the benefit of experiencing God. Rich did not. My experience with God allowed me an understanding of total life. Rich was looking at life from the viewpoint of living and dying. But life with death is only half the equation of life. Life has two parts. The first part of life is life with dying. The second part of life is life without dying.

So how do you play the game of life? In order to play the game you need to know the rules, but more than the rules you need to understand why you're playing. The game of life was designed by God. In Isaiah 43:7 God says, "everyone who is called by my name, whom I created for my glory, whom I formed and made." In

Revelations 4:11 God says, "Thou art worthy, O Lord, to receive glory and honor and power: for thou hast created all things, and for thy pleasure they are and were created." It would appear then that God has created Team Human for his joy and pleasure and to give him glory. So, if you're God and you have no beginning or no ending and you have always existed, I would guess that existing forever can get very lonely. So we play the game of life to please God and give him glory.

Just as life has two parts, so do members of team human. Team Humans have a physical part and a spiritual part or soul. The game of life was designed to use both the physical and spiritual aspects while playing the game of life.

It is interesting how life can be a little humorous at times. I ran into Rich during an interview for a position I was applying for as an engineering geologist. Rich, along with two other people, was a member of my interview panel. Rich and I had a few other issues besides the soul one. During Rich's master's defense, some twenty-plus years before, I took issue with his mapping of a camping area in the San Bernardino Mountains, called Broom Flats, as a landslide. I did a very good job at shooting down some very important aspects of his evidence for a landslide.

Back to the interview. The first words out of Rich's month were "So, Mr. Feay, tell me why Broom Flats should be mapped as a landslide." I did not get the position for engineering geologist, which was a shame because the office I wanted to go to was only seven miles from my home, while the office I wanted to leave was 100 miles from my home.

Rules

The rules can seem a little confusing. This is due to the fact that there are three sets of rules. The first set of rules is written in stone and apply to all members of Team Human equally. The first set of rules is very simple. Set one rule one: every team member is drafted into Team World at birth. Set one rule two: every team member exits the game of life via death's doorway with no prior notice. Set one rule three: upon exiting life's game, you enter the second half of the game of life on the team you were rostered on when you exited the first half of the game. Set one rule four: you can only use the free agent contract to change teams during the first half of life. These rules are not changeable and apply to all team members equally.

The second and third set of rules depend on which team you are on while playing the game of life. There are two teams that play the game of life and they play in a stadium called the universe. Team World is managed by an angel named Lucifer. God has given Lucifer complete control of Team World, even to the point of controlling all the rules for Team World. Why God put Lucifer in charge of Team World has been a mystery to me. Lucifer would not have been my choice to manage Team World. Lucifer has decided that there are no rules for his team.

That is because Lucifer does not care about team members. All he wants is to hurt God. Remember team members were created for God's joy and pleasure. Anything Lucifer can do to separate God from team members he will do. The Bible says in First Peter 5:8, "Be sober, be watchful: your adversary the devil, as a roaring lion, walketh about, seeking whom he may devour." Lucifer was created by God on the second day of creation or, by the twenty-four-hour standard, about 9 billion years ago. Lucifer has lots of experience in dealing with and deceiving team members.

The next team, Team God, is managed by God's son Jesus. The third set of rules for Team God were written by God. Team God has two rules. Mark 12:29-31 says, "Jesus answered them saying, The most important is, Hear, O Israel: The Lord our God, the Lord is one. And you shall love the Lord your God with all your heart and with all your soul and with all your mind and with all your strength. The second is this: You shall love your neighbor as yourself. "There is no other commandment greater than these." So these are the only rules that count. Team God has also given his team members a coach, the Holy Spirit, to guide and advise. Remember I said that when you are born you are placed on Team World's roster? If you decide to change teams during the first half of the game of life, you can. You do this by exercising the free agency contract. Team God's manager will admit you to Team God just by changing your loyalty (heart). You ask Jesus to change your heart and forgive you for all the rules that you broke while on Team World. John 3:16 and 17 says, "For God so loved the world, that he gave his only Son, that whoever believes in him should not perish but have eternal life. For God did not send his Son into the world to condemn the world, but in order that the world might be saved through him."

The Stadium

The first half of the game of life is played in the physical universe that God created. The second half of the game of life is played in one of two places. Those two places are heaven and hell. The stadium for these two places is located outside the physical universe. It is interesting to note that the creator of the game of life gives us about 80 years to play the first half and forever to play the second. The next question, then, is why there are two parts to the game of life. The game of life did not always have two parts. In the beginning God first created a garden for Team Human to live in. We were to enjoy life with God in the garden forever, but we broke the rules that God set up for us to live by. So God tossed us out of the garden and set up the game of life with two parts. God would like a relationship with us that will last forever. The only way that is possible now is in the second half of the game of life played in Heaven.

To get to Heaven you must be on Team God when you exit the first half of life's game. Remember you were born onto the Team World's roster. So in order to join Team God, you must exercise the free agency contract.

This can only be done in the first half of life's game. This means that we have about 80 years to make one decision. Lucifer, through Team World, will do everything in his power to keep us from exercising the free agency contract. About 32 percent of the world's population say they are Christian. That means that 68 percent of the population belongs to Team World. So 68 percent will, by default of the rules, have to spend their second half of the game of life in Hell. So what does Hell really look like?

Hell

Lucifer has greatly confused Team World's viewpoint on Hell so that they believe it is not that bad of a place or that Heaven is not that great. When I was about thirteen, I found one of my uncle Ken's *Playboy* magazines. I was only reading it for the cartoons. Uncle Ken was a very interesting team member. He worked for KTLA in their news van and also made movies. One day he showed up at our house with a news van full of bullet holes. He was reporting on the Symbionese Liberation Army's (SLA) fight with the Los Angeles police. His news van was between the police and the SLA, and he was getting gunfire from both sides. After that day, I was talked into helping Ken make movies. I was free labor. The work was fun and I got free lunch. A few years later, Uncle Ken died of acute alcoholic poising. My dreams of a career in the movie industry died with him. Getting back to Hell, the cartoon showed a man being asked to choose his punishment. He chose to be put with a group of team members who were drinking wine while walking around knee-deep in sewage. The last frame of the cartoon showed a demon yelling out, "Ok, your break is over. Everyone back down on your hands." This idea of Hell belongs to Team Human. But what does the Bible say?

The Bible only has fourteen references to Hell. Here is what one says. Luke 16:19-26: "There was a rich man who was clothed in purple and fine linen and who feasted sumptuously every day. And at his gate was laid a poor man named Lazarus, covered with sores, who desired to be fed with what fell from the rich man's table. Moreover, even the dogs came and licked his sores. The poor man died and was carried by the angels to Abraham's side. The rich man also died and was buried, and in Hades, being in torment, he lifted up his eyes and saw Abraham far off and Lazarus at his side. And he called out, Father Abraham, have mercy on me, and send Lazarus to dip the end of his finger in water and cool my tongue, for I am in anguish in this flame. But Abraham said, Child, remember that you in your lifetime received your good things, and Lazarus in like manner bad things; but now he is comforted here, and you are in anguish. And besides all this, between us and you a great chasm has been fixed, in order that those who would pass from here to you may not be able, and none may cross from there to us."

From the passage we can learn several things about Hell. First thing is that your position in the game of life has no effect on where you end up. A very wealthy man went to Hell, while a very poor man went to heaven. I think it safe to say that the rich man's heart was focused only on himself. Being rich in those days suggests that the rich man was smart. But his head and heart were not connected. All brains, no heart. It's like having a 65-inch 4K television and not hooking it up to the signal from the input box. You need an HDMI cable between the TV and input box in order to have a complete system that works. The same can be said for getting a complete system that works so Team Human members can connect with God. Only Jesus can hook your heart and head together so you can understand and relate to God. John 14:6 "Jesus said to him, I am the way, and the truth, and the life. No one comes to the Father except through me." Without Jesus no one gets to heaven.

I have always wondered what happens when you pass from the first part of life to the second part. Here it is clear that the poor man with a great heart went straight to heaven, while the rich man with no heart went to hell and suffered a lot.

We can also see in this story that Hell has no water. Just think about having no water. It does not seem like much until you remember the night before, when you got up in the middle of the night because your mouth was so dry it hurt. You reach over and take a cool drink of water and go back to sleep, only to wake up and do the water thing all over again. Now imagine not being able to quench your thirst ever. You have the dry, hurting mouth and no water ever. It is also not hard to imagine that there is no food in Hell either.

At this point you might be thinking that food and water are not all that important because your soul is spirit, not flesh. That is true, but when you pass from the first part of life to the second, you will receive a new body. That new body is not spirit. Luke 24:40-43 says, "and as they spake these things, he himself stood in the midst of them, and saith unto them, Peace be unto you. But they were terrified and affrighted, and supposed that they beheld a spirit. And he said unto them, Why are ye troubled? and wherefore do questionings arise in your heart? See my hands and my feet, that it is I myself: handle me, and see; for a spirit hath not flesh and bones, as ye behold me having. And when he had said this, he showed them his hands and his feet. And while they still disbelieved for joy, and wondered, he said unto them, have ye here anything to eat? And they gave him a piece of a broiled fish. And he took it, and ate before them." Jesus was the first to get the new body when he rose from the dead. His new body was solid and he needed to eat. The difference between this body and the one that died is that this new body does not die. The new body lives forever.

I see in the parable that there is no way of ever getting out of Hell once you're there. I can only wonder at how large the great chasm is that is mentioned in the parable. I have seen the Grand Canyon, and if the chasm is bigger, forget about ever escaping from Hell. In talking about the great chasm, the Bible uses the words "it has been fixed." I'm sure whatever God has done to "fix" the great chasm, there is no way it can be undone.

The inability to leave Hell means that all team members who end up in Hell will forever be in a state of hopelessness. Hopelessness is something that is very foreign to most team members. During the first half of life, the world is always telling you that there is always hope. Hey, you could win the lotto. Just work hard and all things will work out fine. Or there is always welfare. Everywhere you look, you will always find that there is hope. You see where there is life, there is hope. But only during the first half of the game of life does hope exist for all. On the second half of life's game, hope only exists in Heaven. The one place where hope does not exist is Hell. "And if anyone's name was not found written in the book of life, he was thrown into the lake of fire." Revelations 20:14

Heaven

So what is Heaven like? The Bible has 422 references to Heaven. In Revelation 21:14, there is a description of a new Heaven. Eventually everyone in the book of life will end up here. "The wall was built of jasper, while the city was pure gold, like clear glass. The foundations of the wall of the city were adorned with every kind of jewel. The first was jasper, the second sapphire, the third agate, the fourth emerald, the fifth onyx, the sixth carnelian, the seventh chrysolite, the eighth beryl, the ninth topaz, the tenth chrysoprase, the eleventh jacinth, the twelfth amethyst. And the twelve gates were twelve pearls, each of the gates made of a single pearl, and the street of the city was pure gold, like transparent glass." Chapter 22, verses 1 to 5 give a very unique look at the new heaven. "And he showed me a river of water of life, bright as crystal, proceeding out of the throne of God and of the Lamb, in the midst of the street thereof. And on this side of the river and on that was the tree of life, bearing twelve manner of fruits, yielding its fruit every month: and the leaves of the tree were for the healing of the nations. And there shall be no curse anymore: and the throne of God and of the Lamb shall be therein: and his servants shall serve him; and they shall see his face; and his name shall be on their foreheads. And there shall be night no more; and they need no light of lamp, neither light of sun; for the Lord God shall give them light: and they shall reign for ever and ever." This description of the new Heaven gives us a glimpse of where all the team members who are in the game of life will be spending the second half of life. I can't imagine anyone choosing to spend forever in Hell when Heaven is available. Yet team members pass into the second half of life daily not choosing Heaven.

Hell or Heaven – Your Choice

Choice is something that everybody wants. The right to choose is in our genes. The first half of life is all about choice. There are no choices in the second half of life, only Heaven or Hell.

The world is full of choices that in the end will let you down and eventually lead to Hell. For example, there is a lot of pseudo brain science in the world which says if you get your brainpower to maximum, you will be perfect. Doing this will cause your heart to become disconnected from your brain, and your ego will take over and it will cost you. Your ego will engage, and you will forget God and live forever in Hell. Not a very good decision on your part. At the other end of the scale exist the "all you need is love" team members. They're the ones with the "COEXIST" bumper sticker. It is a nice idea, but human love does not last. Lucifer was the one who probably started the rumor about love. God's love, unlike Team Human's love, lives on forever and will never fail. Look at the poor man in the story. God loved him enough to take him to Heaven even though his life on earth had a lot of bumps.

Lucifer is smarter than any team member and has been around since Heaven was created. He has a way of stealing your soul, "soul-jacking," and you will not even know it's gone until you're dead. Everyone has a soul, and that soul is known by the spiritual group they hang with. If you don't hang with Jesus's group, then by default you're with Lucifer. A life rule that can never be altered is that if you do not choose to follow Jesus, you belong to Lucifer. There are no exceptions to this rule of life. So then the question becomes: where do you plan on spending forever, in Hell or Heaven?

Chapter Five

Jesus: "Who Do You Say I Am?"

The Bible contains 353 prophecies about Jesus. These prophecies were written about 600 years before he was born. A professor at Westmont College calculated the odds it would take to fulfill just 48 prophecies at 10 to the 157 power. That is 10 with 157 zeros after it. Another way to visualize it would be to drop a ping pong ball painted black onto the state of Texas. Then cover the entire state with white ping pong balls three feet deep. Now jump out of an airplane and land on the state of Texas and reach down through the three feet of ping pong balls and pick up the black ping pong ball. The odds of you coming up with the black ping pong ball would be about the same as a man fulfilling 353 prophecies written 600 years before his birth. Yet that is what Jesus did. The most unique person to ever be born was Jesus. His birthplace, life and death, and resurrection were all predicted about 600 years before his birth. His resurrection was witnessed by over 500 hundred people.

Why was it necessary to sacrifice Jesus? Because we (Team Human) chose not to except God's gift of life in a fantastic garden. Then God said, "Okay, I choose the nation of Israel to lead man to me." Israel rejected God's law and his gifts. God had no choice but to sacrifice his son for the love of Team Human. Isaiah 7:14 says, "Therefore the Lord himself will give you a sign: behold, a virgin shall conceive, and bear a son, and shall call his name Immanuel." Mark 1:9-11 "And it came to pass in those days, that Jesus came from Nazareth of Galilee, and was baptized of John in the Jordan. And straight-way coming up out of the water, he saw the heavens rent asunder, and the Spirit as a dove descending upon him: And a voice came out of the heavens, Thou art my beloved Son, in thee I am well pleased." Mark 8:29-31: "And he asked them, But who say ye that I am? Peter answered and saith unto him, Thou art the Christ. And he charged them that they should tell no man of him. And he began to teach them, that the Son of man must suffer many things, and be rejected by the elders, and the chief priests, and the scribes, and be killed, and after three days rise again."

All members of Team Human need to understand that there is nothing more important in the first half of life than to make a decision one way or the other as to one's relationship to Jesus.

To all my very special Jewish families, please research the prophecies and find out for yourself if Jesus is the messiah. Jesus will not make you less Jewish, he will complete your Jewish heart. You will be as God intended you to be, a completed Jew. Check out a group called Jews for Jesus. They are fantastic.

Chapter Six

Death From God's Point of View

My first experience with death came in the third grade. Our teacher, Ms Coldwell, was walking the class to nutrition break when she suddenly fell over and rolled to the bottom of the stairs. She was very blue in color, almost matching her blue dress. Ms Coldwell only wore a dark blue or black dress and never used deodorant. My next close encounter came on a Greyhound bus. I was on the bus going from San Francisco to Los Angeles. I was thirteen years old. I had just spent the summer in Twin Falls with my mother's sister. I started riding the bus from Los Angeles to Twin Falls when I was twelve years old. I guess you could say I was raised a free-range kid. Anyway, getting back to the bus ride, an older woman got on the bus in Santa Barbara and took the seat next to me. We started talking and after a while she got very quiet. I, however, continued to talk, all the way to Los Angeles. The bus pulled into the station and people began to leave the bus. The lady next to me never got up. I also saw that the cigarette in her hand had burned down and was melting the skin on her hand. I thought that she was one tough woman. I touched her shoulder to get her attention, with no response. I tried again and still no response. Her eyes were wide open and staring straight ahead. By the time the bus had emptied, I had figured the lady was dead. I went and got the bus driver and told him that the lady in the seat next to me had died. He did not believe me. He thought I was playing a joke on him. I got him to go look at the lady. When he got to the seat, he touched her shoulder and she fell out of the seat onto the floor. The bus driver made an interesting noise and jumped back. With that I left the bus driver and the dead lady. I could hear the bus driver yelling at me to come back. I yelled back that my dad was waiting for me.

After Vietnam I was sent to Letterman General Hospital. After working in several different areas of the lab I finally ended up in the morgue. About 400 autopsies later, I had a very good appreciation for the dead. So when over 500 people saw Jesus after his resurrection, I have a much greater respect and understanding for just how impossible rising from the dead is. But God seems to always do the impossible.

Jesus said this about death: John 11:11-15, "After saying these things, he said to them, Our friend Lazarus has fallen asleep, but I go to awaken him. The disciples said to him, Lord, if he has fallen asleep, he will recover. Now Jesus had spoken of his death, but they thought that he meant taking rest in sleep. Then Jesus told them plainly, Lazarus has died, and for your sake I am glad that I was not there, so that you may believe. But let us go to him." Why had Jesus used the word sleep instead of the word death? Jesus (God) looks at death as if a team member just fell sleep. To God there is no death, just sleep. Jesus was the perfect example of what happens after you die. He rose from the dead and took on a new body that will never die. When a team member wakes up, they will also have a new body. It is extremely important to understand that death is just sleep.

I love to read books and watch movies about science fiction. Over the last fifty years there have been thousands of stories about living forever. Team members are obsessed with not dying. Guess what, God has already taken care of the living-forever thing. Every team member from Adam on gets a new body after waking from death. The question is where the team member will spend forever. With Team Jesus in heaven or with Team Lucifer in the lake of fire.

Chapter Seven

Something To Think About

I was watching a movie called "Ready Player One" and was struck by the idea that the movie reflected the reality of the relationship between our physical being and our soul.

In the movie, the main character lives in one world and moves to a second world via an avatar. The main character needs his avatar in order to live in the second world. Team Human members each have a soul. Our soul is in the image of God. In Genesis 1:27 "So God created mankind in his own image…" God is a spirit. Only Jesus has human form. So if God is a spirit, then what part of mankind is in the image of God? It is our soul. Our soul is spiritual in nature. The only way our soul can exist or function in this world is through the avatar of our physical bodies. The soul needs to be in communication with God. The only way for that to happen is through a physical relationship with Jesus. The choice is yours, but remember, when you die, and you will, your soul (spirit) will no longer be bound by your physical body (avatar) and will go back to God. There are only two places for

God to send your soul for the rest of eternity. Those two places are Heaven or Hell; it's your choice.

Jezebel

There is a story in Revelation 2:20. In the church at Thyatira in the province of Asia lived a woman named Jezebel. She called herself a prophet. We don't know much about her spiritual abilities, but they must have been very convincing for God was not happy with what she was doing. God said, "By her teaching she misleads my servants into sexual immorality and eating of food sacrificed to idols." I guess she also blended her spiritual prophecy with some very physical activities. Things have not changed all that much since Jezebel's days. Sex is still used by Lucifer to spread bad ideas and bad information.

There are only two spiritual worlds. One that belongs to God and one that God has given to Lucifer. Since Jezebel was not getting her spiritual information from God, she must have been getting it from Lucifer. Today we would call Jezebel a psychic. Wikipedia lists one of the abilities of a psychic as the ability to predict the future. So what is in store for those who use psychics? God said, "I have given her time to repent of her immorality, but she is unwilling. So I will cast her on a bed of suffering, and I will make those who commit adultery with her suffer intensely, unless they repent of her ways. I will strike her children dead. Then all churches will know that I am he who searches hearts and minds, and I will repay each of you according to your deeds." Jezebel is still suffering in

Hell today. God not only ended her line, but also ended her name. Ask yourself how many women you have met that are named Jezebel. I have never met one. So next time you are inclined to go to a psychic, don't. If you do it, it might lead to a stay in Hell for a very long time. Remember Heaven or Hell are the only two places you can go when you die. And the only way to get to Heaven is through Jesus. In John 14:6 Jesus said, "I am the way and the truth and the life. No one comes to the Father except through me." God gives Team Human members about 77 years to make a decision regarding Jesus. If no decision is made, then by default Hell is where you will end up.

Chapter Eight

Thrift Store Savings

My wife loves a good bargain. If she can save a dollar on something, it is a good day. I must admit that all her savings have come in handy. Thrift stores are high on her list for places to shop. They have treasures that are yet to be discovered. One day she brought home a very cool Hawaiian shirt. My only fear with wearing the shirt is that I will be talking to someone new at church while wearing my Hawaiian shirt, and the woman would say, "My late husband had a shirt just like yours." To which I would reply, "He had great taste in shirts."

Did you know that God likes to shop for lost souls? Souls that the world has discarded. God can take a lost soul and turn it into a fantastic treasure. Below are a few stories, in their own words, from members of my church whom God has turned into treasures.

Gerard Van Hiejzen

The year was 1939. Two young people got engaged. Not long after Hitler thought he would have a run at ruling the world. In April 1940 he invaded the Netherlands. That's where those two young engaged people lived, in

Rotterdam, where Hitler thought it was interesting to drop some of his bombs. They fled to a small village just outside Rotterdam and waited out the war before they decided on a wedding date. Smart. Life was pretty uncertain then. Especially since they were assisting the underground.

One interesting occasion occurred when they were helping the underground people smuggle loads of ration cards. Traveling by bike they met a German patrol checking bikes along their route. Oops, not a chance to turn around without suspicion. Without saying a word to each other, these two smugglers both raised their arms in Nazi style and declared 'Heil Hitler' and passed the patrol without a second look.

With the war finally over they could now think about life again. They got married and had two girls sometime later. They wanted more children, but nothing happened.

They were devout people and believed in the One and Only God of the Bible, so they prayed a bit like Hannah did in the Old Testament: "Lord, please give us a child. You can take the child wherever you want him to go." That child was me. I entered the world.

Fast forward a bit. I was not interested in any type of religion. The schools I attended were so-called Christian schools. One was called "School with the Bible." I am still trying to figure out where that Bible was because I never saw it. I was probably deaf and blind, but I cannot remember ever hearing the Gospel until I was eighteen.

Two of my friends had recently become Christians and told me I needed to become a Christian too or I would go to Hell. They were right on, but I told them, "Religion is for old people." The church in my hometown was originally built around 1430 and it seemed to me the charter members were still in the pews. Boring and old-fashioned is what I thought of it. Give me the Doors, Led Zeppelin, and all the rock artists of the sixties and early seventies.

But, one day, a light went on. Perhaps I might not get old. God did exist. I somehow knew that. The Bible was God's Word. I somehow knew that too, but I was not a believer.

Sometime in February 1973, a friend, Andre, told me about his troubles. So I did what all good unbelievers do, and I told him that the Jesus thing would be good for him. He became a believer. That had me thinking. Something is wrong here. Believing this was good for someone else, but not for me does not seem right. The next day I accepted the Lord as Savior of my life.

After graduation from high school, I was drafted as a military policeman but did not want to go. They sent me to Germany. Again I did not want to go. They put me on a motorbike. I did not want to go. But you could not say no without some negative consequences from the Dutch government. So I did as I was told.

After military, some friends wanted to attend a Bible school in Brussels, Belgium. I had a car. They did not. They asked me to drive them to Belgium. I did. When they did their interviews, I wondered what to do with my time. I knew I wanted to serve the Lord. So I did an interview as well and got accepted. I spent three years in Belgium. A wonderful young lady had graduated from Biola College in California and got a position with Greater Europe Mission as a music teacher at a Bible school. She was going to France. But a last-minute change sent her to Brussels. They had an opening. She decided to take the challenge and one year before I arrived in Brussels, she was there.

I joined a music group she was leading. And fell in love. Two years later in 1977, we got married in California. Our first year as a married couple was spent in Belgium so I could finish school. Having received my diploma, the question was "Now what?" I became a Bible teacher at the public schools in Holland.

Two years later, we felt the Lord tugging our hearts to go to the USA so I could attend Talbot Seminary for a master's degree and also get to know her family and country. When I told my mom (Dad had passed away a month after we got married) that we wanted to move to the USA, she was not surprised. That was the first time she told me about the prayer described above. Don't tell me prayer does not make a difference. I believe it determined my life.

We now have two wonderful children, both married, and they have a combined total of seven grandkids for us. Always nice, but expensive around Christmas time. We love them a lot.

I have seen many answers to prayer. Not just the kind where we ask God to bless our food, and we can say that we are really blessed and healthy because of the meal. I mean some impossible situations. Here is one. My wife and I lived in Vietnam, 1999-2000. We were teachers/missionaries with English Language In China and taught at the Agricultural University of Hanoi. The university was about six miles outside the main city in a very rural area. We were surrounded with rice paddies. I also taught one class in the old part of Hanoi. It was close to Christmas time and the head of the school had asked me to play Santa Claus for their Christmas party. Now, I was surprised by the idea that communist-Buddhist people would even think of celebrating Christmas, but they did. I think they thought any reason to have a get-together and drink would do. I said yes. I was told I had twenty minutes to say what Santa would do.

A couple of days before the event, I got food poisoning, which was not uncommon there in an area where we would probably rate the restaurants at F-. I even went to the hospital to get some help. On the afternoon of the event I still felt sicker than a dog, so, instead of riding my bike as I usually did, I hired a motorbike taxi. We stopped at the post office to pick up a package from the USA. I communicated with the taxi driver when and where he was to pick me up and off he went. I walked the rest of the way. Mistake. Dragging my feet through the streets of Hanoi, I constantly prayed, "Lord, I cannot do this. Help." I could not back out either. Losing face is an important concept there and the leader would lose face if Santa would not show up. Dragging my feet upstairs to the office, I sat down and continued to pray. There was the dreaded Santa suit, beard and all. The leader walked in and we communicated about the timing once again. "You want me to play Santa for about twenty minutes, right?" "Oh no, you have the whole evening, two hours." My heart went to the bottom floor again and left me just sitting there trying to smile and figure out how this would work and pray. "Help."

Time to put on the suit. Almost seven p.m. Between sixty and seventy communist-Buddhists would be sitting there to wait for the man from the North Pole.

I was still praying and feeling terrible. Getting up, I walked to the door for this awful moment. But God is real and He is in charge. I opened the door, and the moment I crossed the threshold I was completely well. No more weakness, no more aches, nothing. Just plain well. As Santa, I even got a chance to tell them that Christmas is not really about Santa, but about a little baby born in Bethlehem, Whose Name is Jesus. And they did not arrest me or kick me out. The Bible tells us to always pray and to pray about all things (Phil. 4). That means praying about your food is not a bad idea.

Many years ago I was discipling a young man. He had just become a Christian and I was asked to help him grow in the Lord. We met once a week and usually had a time of questions to help him with the more difficult parts of the Bible he had been thinking about that week.

This time he had a great one. "God knows all things, right?" "Yup." "And He has everything under His control, right?" "Yup again." "Then why do we pray?" Great question! Why do we pray? Several thoughts came to mind.

First, there is the simple answer. We are commanded to pray in the Bible. Jesus tells us to pray (Matthew 6). Paul tells us to pray in several different places, like 1 Thess. 5 and Phil. 4. I would think a command from the God of heaven and earth would in itself be enough to make us do something. We actually like to follow rules. If you do not believe that, just watch a sports event where a referee makes a wrong call. We love rules, especially when others are required to follow them.

We should pray always and for all things, including the little things of life. Paul tells us to pray without ceasing, no stopping, no breaks. But as we all know, that is humanly impossible. We cannot do two cognitive things 100% at the same time. One or the other must give. Praying is a cognitive thing. I think then that Paul means we must always have an attitude of prayer and readiness to pray. But we must pray in faith, not just rattle off some words and be done with it. Prayer is effort. It can even be a battle for you.

A second reason we should pray is because God is our Father. Fathers and children have relationships. We need to develop a relationship with God. Once we are born again (John 3), we are children of God (John 1:12). Part of our responsibility as children is to talk to our heavenly

Father. God will not change His plans because of my prayers. But He will want me to talk with Him about all things of life. If you have children, you understand that quite well. Prayer, then, is to change us, not God's plans or will. Thus we can say that if God answered our prayer, we in actuality finally learned to line up with His will and plans for the circumstances we prayed about.

It is not easy to understand God. We may still be stuck with the idea of "why do we pray then?" Somewhere in all of this we do also have a certain amount of freedom. And God wants us to use that to learn to make right decisions. I have noticed that there are things that I can do and God will not. I will not go as far as "God helps those who help themselves," but when I look at Scripture, I see Jesus interacting with people on this level. Take the story of Lazarus, John 11. Lazarus had been dead for four days. The tomb was a cave with a stone rolled in front of it. It is said about Jesus that He is the Creator of the universe (John 1, Col. 1, Hebr. 1), God in the flesh (Phil. 2, Hebr. 1, John 1, John 10, John 14, John 18). He could easily have moved the stone and shown His power that way as well. He did not. He told the people to move the stone. That showed their faith. Then Jesus did what people could not do. He said, "Lazarus, come forth" and raised him back to life. Now it was up to the people again to do the rest, to get the grave clothes off and regular clothes on the man. I see this in many of the Biblical stories. Jesus does the impossible, miraculous, when people do what part they can.

Keep on praying about all things, but don't ask God to provide food for you when you are unwilling to work. The Bible says it this way: "If a man will not work, he shall not eat," 2 Thess. 3:10. Thus, "work and pray" is a good maxim. Keep up the good work.

Ryan Low

My name is Ryan and I've become a Christian maybe a hundred times in my life! I know that may sound strange but hopefully it will make sense.

This year I turned 44, which marks 30 years I've been a follower of Jesus Christ. Some people might look at my entire life story and say: "Well, of course you became a Christian and have been so ever since," but hold on, it hasn't been that easy.

I was born to a Christian family that attended church. Some folks might say: "Yes, Ryan, the reason you are a Christian is because it's all you've ever known. You're not making a brave stand for God more than you are afraid to imagine a world without Him. It's all conditioning, man… you grew up in a world that pushed you towards Christianity, and so naturally you went that way, nothing special there."

And if I'm to be humble, I must admit you may be right. I may have some conditioning in me, but then again, don't we all? In reflecting on my younger years, though, I sometimes wonder if the world I grew up in actually pushed me towards Christ.

The truth is, I did grow up in a Christian home

although for many of my growing-up years, neither of my parents were ever really that demonstrative with their faith. My parents were and are awesome people (please don't misunderstand), but when I was a kid, we weren't really much different from any other family on my street who didn't attend church. It wasn't until my teen years I began to see a Christian faith in my mother. My father didn't really come to follow the Lord until several years after that. So let me just give you my perception of Christianity as I was growing up.

It was church. I didn't see Christianity as a friendship with God. I saw it as an event I went to two or three times a month, on Sundays, when I'd rather be home playing with my friends. We called this event "Church," but I really saw it as Christianity.

Christianity was: Stuffy suits with uncomfortable ties, being forced to sit for a long time, listening to boring music and boring sermons.

It was a church lobby that smelled like old people. I'm sorry if that offends some people, but the truth is that's what I thought.

It was a place full of people who didn't inspire me to become a Christian. That's not to say there weren't wonderful people there, but I was young and didn't know any better, and there was a lot of brokenness in our church. There were some folks who were just flat out unkind, unethical, and racist. There didn't seem to be a lot of powerful change going on. It was really rather unattractive in many ways.

Suffice it to say, the church felt very empty, dull, and hypocritical to me. It was a place I was forced to go to, and it didn't feel like there was real life there. So, to recap, my family was kind of a nominal church-attending family, there wasn't heavy pressure to follow Jesus, there still isn't, and I went to a church that didn't really paint an inspiring portrait of Christianity.

These three facts alone are reasons for many people I've met to choose to simply walk away from religion altogether when they grew up. They went out there and found something they felt was a better fit for them and then ditched the church and "religion" for those things, or they just decided to adopt a belief that there is some kind of powerful "man in the sky" out there and He either doesn't care or we can't know Him so why bother? I guess I'm trying to say: Me becoming a Christian was never really a foregone conclusion even though I grew up going to church.

You add to this the fact that I grew up in a very affluent area of the country. My parents worked hard to make ends meet. My dad would often work two jobs and as a result, we never really experienced the struggles of poverty. While this is a wonderful blessing, it also comes with some difficulties. I was able to taste a moderate level of wealth and prosperity. This isn't bad, but it has a pull to it. It draws you in and tells you life is best and worthwhile this way. The problem is that Christianity doesn't bash wealth but it does warn that the love of money can be destructive. I grew up in a world that says the opposite. The world around me actually pushed me towards living for pleasure, wealth, comfort, prosperity, influence, and basically living for myself. It seemed to me Christianity was teaching the opposite.

So here I am, in a family that doesn't really practice the Christian faith beyond simply going to church a couple times a month, going to a church that wasn't painting a very inspiring picture of Christianity, and living in a world that tells me to love and live for things that are the opposite of what Christianity teaches. It seems much more likely to me that I would be an agnostic or atheist than a Christian. In many ways, I felt like Christianity was out of touch with the greater reality of the world we live in and I was quite ashamed or embarrassed of it.

Why in the world did I become a Christian… and why have I remained so?

When I was fourteen, we went to church camp. It was a cold, snowy night in the mountains and we were huddled indoors, several hundred of us, listening to a man tell us the story of Jesus. To this day I couldn't tell you the guy's name, and I remember very little of what he said except that we needed Jesus to have peace with God. He described how we as humans are separated from God because of our sin, that we would always remain so, and that is why God sent His son to die on a cross for our sins so that we could be brought back together with Him.

I remember sitting in that group, listening to this

man talk about how Jesus died for me and how He did it so I wouldn't have to go to Hell. I remember thinking: "Dude, Hell is going to suck. I need to be sure I don't go there."

At the end of this guy's speech, he invited anyone forward who wanted to come to pray and ask Jesus to be their Lord and Savior. In true businesslike fashion, I decided I had a deal I needed to work out with God that night. It was a very simple transaction, really. Walk forward, pray the prayer, get everything squared away with God, then go back to life as usual. That's all.

I walked forward and did what I needed to do. I remember there were other kids up there crying and going through these deep emotional experiences, but I wasn't experiencing any of that. It was just a really calm and collected moment. "Jesus, I need you so I won't go to Hell. Thanks for dying for me, that's pretty awesome… so yeah, we're good, right? Ok, see you when I die."

That was something I had mistaken in that moment. You see, I thought this was all about me sealing up my fate when I died. It was like I was giving God my afterlife. Ok, Lord, you can have me after I die, but I'll take care of this life I have until then. I still didn't really understand that God wanted more than what I thought He did.

Not much changed about my life after that night in the mountains. I didn't have a radical conversion story where I was on drugs and when I became a Christian I was delivered. I don't have a story of me just being a completely different person. I actually came home from camp and I was still the same guy. I went to church but was still bored. I was still looking forward to being wealthy and living for my own desires. I had a dirty mouth and a dirty mind even after my prayer, so I really wasn't different, which would make me like a lot of people who go to these big rallies and get saved.

I was fully prepared and looking forward to living life on my own terms, but God had different plans.

As I said, I wasn't really different at all when I came home, except there was this little flicker of curiosity. There was a part of me that was genuinely grateful to God that I was saved, and the youth group I was going to was inviting me to step a little further with this faith that I had. I started reading the Bible and going to church on a pretty on-and-off basis. Whenever I didn't have sports obligations, I would go and slowly, somehow, things began to grow in me. I began to pray and found that at times, there was insight and comfort there. I also began to read the Bible, which was boring for me at first, but then there were these moments where something rocked me. I'd be reading and it was like the words jumped out of the page at me. Often these words would inspire, comfort, or challenge me. This would continue with me through my college years and young adulthood. I would go on to get involved with the youth ministry at my church and my interest would grow, but there was always something lurking.

I had these doubts and questions. God, are you actually there? Is this whole Christianity thing something that is for people who are fools or just mentally lazy? Am I just wanting to self-medicate with a dose of hope in a world that actually has none? And what about the other religions? Lord, what do I do with the fact that sometimes you don't seem like a very likable kind of person? Lord. I'm not always inspired by you, and that's weird for me. Like, I'm more inspired by William Wallace from the movie "Braveheart" than I am by you. I could look back over my life and find that there were some wonderful benefits Christianity brought me, but I had these nagging doubts.

To make matters more challenging, I've never seen myself as a very deep thinker or a philosopher. I didn't read these kinds of books, and whenever I tried I'd get lost within a few pages and just give up. So basically, I had become a Christian, but there were significant intellectual blocks in me as well as spiritual. I would struggle on and off in my twenties and thirties with Christ, but I began to learn and in that learning, my faith was rekindled.

During those years, I truly believed God allowed me to come across some speakers like men named Jerry Root and Ravi Zacharias, and the writings of CS Lewis. Later on, He would bring other writers to me like Josh McDowell, Gregory Boyd, Paul Copan, William Lane Craig, Lee Strobel, Timothy Keller, Gary Habermas, and John Lennox. These men worked hard to show that Christianity wasn't just a feel-good religion that served as an opiate to the masses, but a worldview that had significant philosophical, intellectual, and rational backbone to it. They would take some of the biggest questions and challenges brought against Christianity, and they would reasonably and rationally defend the faith with strong precision and power. I found that I would encounter a question like "How can a loving God permit suffering?" and just be flattened by it and yet, a speech, book, or article would find me and help me think and see not just one side of the argument but both sides. I could see the atheistic side. I have heard it for years, but now I was seeing the Christian answers to these questions.

This all went down during my twenties and thirties, and during those years I also began to wrestle with the fact that a part of me didn't think God liked me very much and I wasn't entirely a huge fan of Him either. My problem was that I still had some major reconstruction in my heart needed because somewhere along the way, I was shown that God is not a gracious, kind, generous and wonderful person. I came into contact with bad religion masquerading as Christianity.

As I was wrestling with my doubts on whether I believed in God's existence, I was wrestling with whether I actually liked Him and He actually liked me. So other writers and mentors came my way to begin painting a different picture of God. One of my most important teachers was the Bible itself. I began to see a different picture of the Jesus I knew as a young man. I began to see an inspiring leader, a brilliant teacher, a man with more power than anyone could explain, and brave beyond belief. I began to realize that Jesus was not some wimpy, passive-aggressive, sniveling doormat, but a powerful king who willingly lays down his life for the ones he loves and then flips the script and defies science to pull off the greatest miracle that has ever been witnessed. I began to see that this guy isn't just worthy of my allegiance but my awe and admiration. I began to be introduced to a God who pursues me, a God who loved me before I ever took a breath and has graciously called me His son.

It's weird, but in many ways, I got saved as a four-teen-year-old, but since then I've had moments where God has saved me again and again. I've had doubts and He has brought me amazing insights. I've struggled and He has given me incredible support. I've had moments where intellectual problems have arisen, and through various means, God has met those questions head on in my life. For all of my emotional problems with God, He has shown me again and again He is for me!

You might say it's obvious that I should become a Christian; after all, I was conditioned by my environment to do just that. But my hope is you will have seen that my world didn't condition me at all for this. After becoming saved, I've had many intellectual, spiritual, and emotional hurdles in my way of remaining a Christian. It's not a foregone conclusion that I have remained one. In fact you might argue it was easier for me to become a Christian than to remain one.

The only explanation I can give is that after all my

searching, all my wrestling, I've found that Jesus most adequately answers the questions my heart is hungering to have answered. God has shown me He isn't afraid of my questions, and if I am open, He is willing to come in and stand in the struggle with me, helping me find answers. I've been a Christian for thirty years and I've been saved hundreds of times by God. Thank God for that!

Scott Brown
Heart of the Canyons • Sunland
sunland@hotc.churc

In the late nineteen-fifties I was born in North Glendale Hospital, the third child and second son of an aviation hydraulic engineer and a suburban housewife. I was lucky enough to have been raised in walking distance from my local Southern Baptist church in Lake View Terrace, California. I spent the years of my youth running around on the church grounds and the Tujunga Wash area, riding ponies, catching snakes, and skinny-dipping in the small ponds of the rock quarry, just being a kid.

At the age of nine years old I accepted Christ in Mrs. Needham's primary class and was baptized. I was active in Royal Ambassadors at Mountain View Baptist Church. At the age of eleven, I was very confused about the Holy Spirit; He was obviously still tugging on my heart's strings. I took this confusion as meaning perhaps my baptism hadn't stuck. I went to Pastor Chuck McClung and asked him if it was possible that I wasn't saved. Pastor Charles explained to me the passage John 10:27-30, "My sheep hear my voice, and I know them, and they follow me. I give them eternal life, and they will never perish, and no one will snatch them out of my hand. My Father, who has given them to me, is greater than all, and no one is able to snatch them out of the Father's hand. I and the Father are one." Pastor McClung agreed to re-baptize me at my request.

At age fourteen, my confusion about Christ's call was as a fog lifting; The Holy Spirit was telling me that He wanted me for ministry or as a missionary. As this was becoming clear to me, I began directing my life to that path. I spent many hours worrying and fearing this decision.

By my sixteenth year, I had decided that I had better plan for my life. I wanted to become a lawyer and wanted to serve my country, I wanted what I wanted, and I knew better than God! I chose a path that led me to the United States Air Force. My path would lead to a commission and a military legal career. I found disillusionment with the legal co-workers I encountered in the Air Force. I was able to rework my career into law enforcement. Yet in a very short time, I found myself retired medically. After extensive rehabilitation with the Veterans Administration, I was able to recharge my career working as a HUD Housing Authority Agent. Late on a very cold December morning, on a HUD complex in Compton, California, I found myself ambushed and shot. This led to my second federal retirement. It's funny, I only had to be shot and retired twice to realize that God still had a better plan for me. But did I listen? Heck no! Just as Jonah ran from God's call to Nineveh, I still ran from my promise to serve God.

In early 1998, my father was diagnosed for a second time with cancer. This time it wasn't caught as early as his first bout was. He was stage 4 "Terminal." His cancer was present in his colon, bladder, and pancreas. I was at a point in my life when I was able to take an extended leave of absence from work where I could make myself available to assist my mom in taking care of my father. My mom and I spent many hours taking care of my father in the last three months of his life. One thing my dad was very good at was reminding me about my commitment that I had made to Christ. My father had been a deacon for several years, and he knew the importance of my commitment to God. It was my father who reminded me that God's Plan "A" is always the best plan to follow, BUT even if you mess that up, God's Plan "B" is always going to be better than your Plan "A". Even though I wasn't the father he was, I could still be the deacon he knew I could be. So I followed those footsteps back to Christ.

I have served in my church now going on ten years as a deacon, office administrator, and Minister of Music. It was accepting these positions that has truly fulfilled my life.

The grace of being a Christian, being a father, being a deacon, being a musician, being an administrator, being in Christ's service, being in my Nineveh is the greatest gift anyone can have on earth. I count these as my greatest triumphs.

Boy, can you imagine how much greater it will be in Heaven? It is beyond my comprehension.

DeRon Jones

My name is DeRon Jones. I was a member of the Los Angeles Fire Department for just under 38 years, and besides being a firefighter, I was also a chaplain with the department for twenty years.

After retirement, I was an associate pastor at Osborne Neighborhood Church for about six years. Both of those last two positions are a testimony to God's faithfulness and to His sense of humor. Let me explain.

Do you remember when you were in school and they gave out awards at graduation? Most likely to succeed, smartest, cutest, best athlete, etc. If they would have given out an award for the person most likely to never speak in public, I would have won that award by a landslide. I grew up with two speech problems. I stuttered horribly. I could not put two words together without stumbling over them. I also had what is called a sibilance, which means when I say anything with an s in it, the air comes out the sides of my mouth and not the front. My father used to tell me I sounded like I had a mouthful of mush. Kids constantly would make fun of me. I would break out in a cold sweat if I thought the teacher was going to call on me.

I was in speech therapy from the third grade through junior high school. So that's how I grew up, afraid to open my mouth. You can imagine what that does for your self-esteem. If it wasn't for being good at sports I'm not sure what would have happened.

When I came to the fire department, not much had changed; they still made fun of me. They used to call me the startled fawn because I would never say anything unless I had to. I just kind of had the deer-in-the-headlights look all the time.

You can see why the idea of public speaking was never on my bucket list. To show you how terrified I really was of anything public, I want to give you one example. This happened before I was a Christian. My father was a firefighter. When he retired, they gave him a retirement dinner. As his son I knew they would ask me to say something. Well, I fretted over that for about a month. How could I get up and speak? Everyone would just make fun of me. What am I going to do? The night of the dinner came, and before you would go into the banquet rooms, they had what is called happy hour. Let's just say I used that time to get as happy as I could before the dinner. In fact, I was so happy, a couple of firemen had to escort me to my seat in thc banquet room. I managed to stumble through a few words, although I don't remember what I said. But I got through it.

So let's fast forward to after I received the Lord. I had been a Christian for about a year and a half, and I was struggling with what God wanted me to do and for direction for my life. When public speaking is not possible, it kind of limits your options for ministry. So on a Wednesday night I prayed a prayer with a friend of mine. I said, "Lord, here's the deal. I'm tired of trying to figure out what to do. If you want me to do something, open the door and I promise I will go through it. If you don't want me to do it, don't open the door. I will never try to break down a door you don't open." Be careful what you promise God. He will test you to see if you mean what you say. That was on Wednesday night. The next Sunday we were going to church. At that time we had an early-service adult Sunday school taught by a guy named Jim. We also had a late service. The pastor met me outside and said Jim's daughter had been in a serious motorcycle accident, and he asked if I would I take his class. Before I could say no, God reminded me of the promise I had just made four days earlier. So what could I do? I said yes. We didn't even go to service that morning. We just went to the car and tried to figure out what I was going to do. God was gracious. All we did in class was pray. We prayed for Andrea, Jim's daughter. We prayed for the family and for the pastor. We prayed for everybody. And I got through it. I said, "Thank you, Lord, you came through, lesson learned. I'm done." Well, God had other plans. We went to the hospital, and Andrea was in a coma. As it turned out, she was in an induced coma for six months. When they finally woke her, she had to undergo a lot of therapy but is doing well today. God is good.

While we were in the hospital Jim said, "I don't know when I'll be able to teach again. You'll have to take the class indefinitely." And I thought, no, I don't. But God reminded me of the promise I made, so I said yes. Later that week I was sitting at my desk and the Lord gave me a lesson. I know it was Him because I just started writing and in about an hour I had this complete lesson and that's not me. So I took it to Sunday school, I read it word for word, or should I say I stuttered through it. But I made it and nobody laughed, which was a miracle.

In the class was a person who heads up our Monday night outreach program called Evangelism Explosion. He came up to me after class and said, "That was a really good message on salvation and you need to share that with our EE class." I'm thinking, what is going on here, Lord? I was afraid to say yes, but more afraid to say no, so I said OK. A few weeks later I read it again in EE class. In that class was our associate pastor. He came up to me afterward and said, "You need to share that from the pulpit." Lord, what have you gotten me into? This is not what I signed up for. But a few weeks later, here I was, reading this lesson from the pulpit. We serve an awesome God. But He wasn't finished with me yet. I was asked to become a chaplain with the fire department, where the main ministry is public speaking, funerals, weddings, and invocations at public events. I reluctantly said yes.

A few years later, we had a fire department helicopter crash. We lost three firefighters and a mother and her son, all being transported to Children's Hospital. The memorial service for the firefighters was being held at the sports arena. Because I was a chaplain and I knew one of the firefighters well, it was my task to deliver a ten-minute eulogy. There were about 3,000 firefighters in the seats, live coverage from all three major networks, and many dignitaries on the platform. As I was about to get up and speak, I couldn't help but reflect on the fact that here I was, a guy who just a few years ago felt he had to get drunk in order to have enough nerve to speak in front of a few firefighters. Now here I was in front of what seemed like the whole world. I delivered that eulogy without a flaw, without any stuttering. We serve an awesome God.

To this day I have never asked to do anything in ministry, but God continues to open doors. I don't know what is next. I still get scared every time I speak in public or do anything new. But I have made a choice in spite of my lack of ability. In spite of my fear, I made a promise to God and I refuse to let my fear dictate my action. If God can use a stumbling, bumbling fool like me, just think what He can do in your life if you are willing to take the risk.

God is waiting to do exceedingly, abundantly more than we can ask or hope for. God wants to bless your service. The God of all Creation wants to knock your socks off. God's waiting to do all these great things. And what is HE waiting for? He is waiting for you to say yes. To say "I will risk it all and trust You." It can be a scary ride at times when you look down, but when you look up, it is so worth it.

To God be the glory.

Prayer

Prayer is something I am very passionate about. One of the most powerful yet underused disciplines that we move in as believers is the area of prayer. I think we would all agree that prayer is important. Prayer changes things, especially the one doing the praying. And I am sure we all have an active prayer life.

But to have a full and rich prayer life, we need to understand all of the <u>different</u> ways that we engage in prayer, the different aspects of what prayer really involves.

When you hear the word prayer, what is the first thing that comes to mind? For most of us, we think of prayer as intercession. Asking God to do something in us or in others, to heal us or direct us, or to handle some situation we are about to engage in. And that is a good thing. God loves to hear what's in our hearts. But we need to understand that prayer is so much more than just crawling up on God's lap and asking Him for stuff.

Prayer, in all its forms, is how we communicate with God. It is a mindset. It should be a way of life that permeates everything we do all day, every day.

Every time we engage in the things of God, that is a part of our prayer life. When we move through the day and engage the Holy Spirit in decisions, we need to make that a part of our prayer life. Prayer is a mindset of being in the presence of God 24/7.

That is why scripture says we should pray without ceasing. What that means is to move, function, and think in the spirit and not in the flesh at all times. I don't think any of us have actually arrived there yet, but our goal should be to have a God presence or a God awareness at all times.

If we do that, then when stuff happens in our life, we will react and make decisions based on Godly principles, not our natural instincts.

The real value in prayer is not in getting what you want from God, but in establishing a relationship with Him that carries over into our personal life and permeates our thinking throughout the day.

Now I know there are some who have the gift of prayer, the burden of prayer, and they spend a great deal of time in prayer. If that is you, I thank God for your prayers; I know they make a difference. But for most of us, or at least I know for me, I am easily distracted. My mind begins to wander; I think about the day, things I have to do, whatever. And I constantly have to bring my mind back to those things I'm praying about.

But when we can think of prayer as more than just intercession, when it becomes a way of life rather than a burden, it changes our whole perspective, it changes our life. In order to do that, we need to expand our understanding of what prayer is. Without going into a lot of detail, I would like to suggest several things that we can do in the morning, throughout the day, and at night that will help us to stay in the presence of God at all times.

1) SPEAK PRAISE, glory, and honor to our Lord and Savior, Jesus Christ. It will change the way you look at your day.

2) CONFESS our sins and shortcomings and repent of them, that we might change course and follow the Holy Spirit's leading.

3) READ THE WORD daily. Reading God's Word is critical to our spiritual survival. As we put God's Word in, the Holy Spirit can bring it out as we need it.

4) INTERCESSION. Think what the Church could be if we prayed every day, not just for physical things, but for lifting each other up that we might walk through the day in the power and direction of the Holy Spirit.

5) LISTEN. "Be still and know that I am God." Most of us are pretty good at talking to God. We just need to get better at taking the time to listen.

6) THANKSGIVING. This is critical to our spiritual well-being. The world lives on the negative,

always wanting more, and it's so easy to get caught up in that mentality. But an attitude of gratitude makes everything enough.

7) SINGING. Singing has a way of lifting our spirits. We can sing to Jesus just about any time. It's hard to be down when you are singing praise songs to Jesus.

8) MEDITATION. We need to notably read God's Word, to meditate on it, and ponder: how does it affect us? Meditating on God's Word is what makes the Scriptures come alive in our own lives.

These are just a few of the ways we can learn to be in prayer or in the presence of God at all times. Most of you know who Martin Luther was. He was the leader of the Reformation that changed the way people look at our access to God. And he had this to say about prayer: "If I fail to spend two hours in prayer each morning, the devil gets the victory through the day. I have so much business, I cannot get on without spending three hours daily in prayer." I mention this because there are two very profound truths in what Martin Luther said here. First, if we don't take the time to start our day in some kind of prayer, then there is a good chance the enemy will have his way in our life that day. It won't necessarily be in big ways, but in the little decisions we get to make that lead to bc choices and bad attitudes. The devil can't take away your salvation, but he can take away your joy and your effectiveness in the Kingdom.

The second thing Martin Luther said is that the more I have to do, the more I need to spend time in prayer in the morning. He's got so much to do that he has to first spend three hours in prayer in order to get it all done. Now I am not saying that we spend three hours a day locked away in our prayer closet, or even two hours a day. But the point Martin Luther was making is that prayer is how we do business with God; it's how we walk in victory throughout the day. Prayer, in all its different forms, is communicating with God and allowing Him to accomplish His agenda through us.

Prayer not only changes things, it's the most powerful component to change us. To change our perspective, our God awareness, our ability to look at things from a Godly perspective and not a worldly perspective. But it does not happen by accident. Each one of us has to decide if we really want to go deeper with the Lord. And if we do, we need to be intentional in accomplishing that goal. If you know Jesus as Lord, your salvation is secure, praise God. But while we still live on this earth, having an active and full prayer life is the difference between walking in victory and just hanging on. God does show us the way, but we have to choose if we want to go deeper in Him.

Debbi Fullington

Both of my parents grew up in Christian homes. I'm not sure exactly how and when they came to know Jesus as their personal Savior. That being said, I also grew up in a Christian home. If the church doors were open, we were there, no exceptions! My mom told me that when I was three or so, I accepted Jesus as my Savior at Vacation Bible School. I don't remember, but here is what I do remember.

I was a good kid, everyone said so (firstborn, rule follower). My parents were proud of how "good" I was. I believed that I was good too, so I was able to discount the times that I was unkind to my brother and sister or when my friends and I would make fun of another friend. Overall, I was pretty good. On Wednesday, December 9, 1964, after dinner, my sister Kat and I started to fight. My favorite weapon was my fingernails. I would dig them into her and then beg her to not tell on me. The fight didn't last long because we had to get ready to go to mid-week Bible study.

While at Bible Study "Uncle Lyle" was teaching us about sin. He referenced Romans 3:23 (I had heard that passage many times and even had it memorized), but for some reason (the Holy Spirit), I realized that "all" meant me too. I remembered how mean I was to Kat and that proved that I was a sinner. Not the kind of thing that I liked to think about myself. Then "Uncle Lyle" told us about Jesus, his love for us, and paying the price for my sin so that I could spend eternity with God. That all fell into place for me that evening. I prayed "the prayer" and that was the beginning of my journey.

I continued to go to church every time the doors were open. My entire world revolved around the church, all of my friends were church friends, and all of the fun activities were at church. I can't say that much had changed for me, but I did have a confidence in my standing with God.

A couple of years later, I was walking around the outside of the church waiting for Sunday School to begin, when I had this very strong sense that God was calling me to serve Him one day at Sunland Neighborhood Church. Not just serve Him, but serve Him by reaching the children in the area. I kind of just filed that away in my memory bank and didn't really think much about it until college. I took some child development classes and started to serve in a big sister program. That was a start.

As a teenager, I couldn't get enough of Jesus. I loved to sing and worship Him, I loved to learn more and more about Him, I was kind of insatiable. I memorized chapters and whole books at a time (my favorite was James). I asked a lot of questions of my youth pastor (I think I might have been pretty annoying). All the while, I also started to question all of the "rules" in Christianity. I felt that I couldn't get satisfactory answers on the "why" questions. All of my life, I was not encouraged to question authority, so this time was a challenge for my family.

In college, I did some pushing and crossing of the

boundaries and discovered, firsthand, what happens when you go against what you know to be true. I started to miss Jesus. It was an ache in my soul, and I knew that I needed to get that intimate relationship with Jesus back. Since everything had always come so easily to me, I expected my return to be easy too…it was not. I had to start all over with new friends, new church environment, new knowledge. I had to fight some battles with the enemy to get back into spiritual growth. Many times in this part of my journey, the enemy blocked my path. I was so determined to regain that intimacy with Jesus that I had once had, I was able to fight the fight. I finally got connected in a good college group that really helped me in my spiritual growth.

A couple of years later, I married a brand-new Christian. We started our little family and were firmly planted right back at Sunland Neighborhood Church. One day, the Christian Education pastor, Scott, asked if I would consider helping out with the Pioneer Girls on Wednesday nights. The Holy Spirit reminded me of my calling back in junior high; I said yes immediately. I loved working with the elementary-aged girls. It was great to be a part of a team to reach these girls. The next year, we were introduced to the AWANA Program. This was a revolutionary program for me to serve in. I found my place! I was able to serve the children of Sunland/Tujunga with the gifts that God had given me. I didn't have to teach. I could be an administrator and enable others to serve well. I saw God use this program to change hundreds of lives over the years. We saw many children come to know Jesus as their personal Savior. I felt God's delight in me and my joy in service. Since I had always felt like an outsider and kind of weird as a kid, I always introduced myself as Debbi; I'm weird and proud of it! I wanted all of the kids to know that their own personal weird was a good thing.

At some point during my time serving in AWANA, I started to rely less on God and the Holy Spirit and more on my abilities to run a good club. This perverted my service to be more for me and the kids than for God (who had given me the gift of this ministry). I knew that it wasn't the way it was supposed to be, but I didn't know how to fix it either. Eventually the AWANA ministry ended for me, and this was a very sad time for me (I had imagined that I would die an old woman in my AWANA uniform).

It was at this time, the end of AWANA for me, that my life started to do a spiral. I was clinically depressed, my marriage was a mess, my understanding of God was warped, and I just wanted to die. The only reason that I didn't kill myself was because I couldn't stand the idea of parents having to explain to the AWANA kids that I had ministered to why I was gone.

I got professional help. My sister came and stayed with me and she helped me maneuver through the mental health and insurance systems. I started to see a therapist (it took several tries to find the right therapist for me) and a psychiatrist, who gave me medication that helped tremendously (I am still on that medication today and thank God for it). So the physical and emotional issues were being addressed, but that still left the spiritual issues that I wasn't addressing. That's where Pastor Duke comes into the picture. He also had struggled with depression at one time in his life, so he did a series of sermons on depression and the Christian. The timing was so perfect (as God's timing always is), I was ready to hear what Duke had to say. The bottom line for me was that I knew that God was good and that He loved everyone; I just didn't believe that He could possibly love me.

My sister and family had been praying for me throughout all of this time. Kat knew that my issue with not believing in God's personal love for me was at the core of the last stronghold of my depression. She had been encouraging me to see things differently. I believe it took over a year before I was ready to address this subject. I was at a Solitude Retreat and Kat had given me a book, "Falling In Love With Jesus." This book helped me to begin to regain the intimacy that I had lost with Jesus. I started to mark in the Book of Psalms every reference to God's unfailing love. I began to see that God's love had everything to do with His character and nothing to do with the behavior of His loved ones. This was revolutionary for me. As I began to trust in His perfect love for me, my life began to open up again.

Serving and ministry have been a privilege for me, but I felt as if I had thrown away that gift and didn't know if I would ever be able to serve again. One day, someone called my office looking for someone to disciple her. I knew that was God giving me a second chance. I didn't know very much about discipleship, but I was ready to go wherever God called me to go. This season of serving has been so rewarding, as He has shown me how many people are in the exact same boat that I was in, questioning God's love for them. God has given me a voice to share His love, and I love doing it.

So, bottom line is that I love Jesus and He loves me.

Lois Seymour

Doug asked me if I would write my testimony for his book. My first reaction was that I don't have a spectacular testimony. You know, those people who have committed murder, done drugs, aborted their babies and other horrible stuff. Not me.

I was raised in a Pentecostal-Holiness Christian home, a very strict one. Now we call these church groups legalistic. No lipstick, nail polish, movies, dancing, bowling, drinking, drugs… you name it, it was a sin. These standards, which I followed (except for bowling), made me a very holy person, or did they? I worked for a business that was owned by a Christian man. He rented a small bowling alley (no liquor), and employees were invited to bowl. I went and enjoyed the bowling and the friendships. My mother was against this and put lots of guilt trips on me. I finally decided to quit, and when I told my mom, she told me she had been praying that I would quit. This was not God convicting me of the "sin" of bowling, but me giving in to my mother to keep peace. It did not make me holy.

God gave us the Ten Commandments in the Old Testament. (Exodus 20:3-17) They are in order, but not by degree of sin. Murder is as much of a sin as coveting. Wow! I would never consider murdering someone, but I might have a problem with coveting. So that makes me a sinner, even if I obeyed all the other commandments and strict rules of my childhood? I didn't think I liked that. After all, I was trying to obey the rules and that would make me a good Christian, or would it?

How about the religious rulers of the temple, at the time of Christ? They considered themselves very holy. Down through the centuries, they embellished the Ten Commandments by adding all kinds of rules and exceptions, called the Traditions of the Elders. They hated Jesus when he broke the Traditions of the Elders. He did not break the Ten Commandments. Jesus and his disciples ate wheat from a field on the Sabbath. Jesus even healed sick people on the Sabbath. He cleansed the temple. He went about challenging the traditions. They killed him!

So how does this affect me and my strict upbringing? I really don't think God cares if I wear lipstick. He does care how I feel about Jesus' death. His death was to save my soul and to help me lead a life that is pleasing to him. By the way, "All have sinned and fall short of the glory of God, and all are justified freely by His grace, through the redemption that came by Christ Jesus." (Romans 3:23-24) So that makes me a sinner who is saved by grace, even if I obeyed the rules of my childhood. I hated being the only girl in high school who did not wear lipstick, but the rules did not hurt me. I no longer feel those rules affect my holiness.

By the way, I have the Holy Spirit in my life, and He convicts me of sin in my life. He does a pretty good job. I just have to listen and stop the sin. Not some silly manmade (traditions) rules that have nothing to do with my commitment to Christ. God has put me in churches that honor God and the Bible. He has brought people into my life who have helped me in my walk with Christ, and He has brought me unconditional love.

Jesus has given us some rules that we can find hard to follow. How about "love your neighbor as yourself" (Matt. 19:19)? Does that include the people who deliberately hurt us, or the neighbor who listens to loud music or whose dog barks all night? Yes!

How about John 13:34? "A new command I give you; love one another. As I have loved you, so you MUST love one another. By this everyone will know that you are my disciples, if you love one another."

My life is to be ruled by love. Not always easy.

My testimony IS spectacular! Not for the sins I have not committed, but for the spectacular life that I have enjoyed as a follower of Christ. He loves me as I allow the Holy Spirit to lead me in all aspects of my life.

E. Jill Bowker

Today I am a confident believer and follower of Jesus

Christ. I know now that He has been watching and wooing me my whole life… even when I didn't care about Him or love Him. He was pursuing me, waiting patiently for me to make that decision when I was ready.

I have a strong relationship with God, Jesus, and the Holy Spirit, and because of that relationship I can live in this crazy world with His peace and comfort, in good times and bad.

Philippians 4:6-7, "Do not be anxious about anything but in every situation by prayer and petition, with thanksgiving present requests to God. And the peace of God will guard your hearts and minds in Christ Jesus."

But I didn't have this amazing relationship with my Creator when I was young. That happened many years later… so let's begin.

My story is a simple one. It's not laden with overcoming drugs, hitting rock bottom because of alcohol addiction, nor does it include an abusive childhood filled with trauma. No, none of that happened to me. Just a normal childhood.

I was the only child of two loving parents who spoiled me rotten with their love and with things. They did love me unconditionally. We were not wealthy, but I never lacked for anything. They were not church people but they somehow decided that I needed to go to church. They took me to the Baptist church down the street… ALL BY MYSELF at eight years old.

I wish I could say that is where my journey with Jesus started. But sadly, it did not. I sat in that church very angry at my parents and at God. I let Him know about it very succinctly; I said, "I hate you, GOD!" My mom and dad still made me go to church during my elementary years and nothing changed my view about God and the church…. Little did I know that seeds were being planted and watered. And God was waiting patiently at the door of my heart for me to let Him in.

Middle school came and went, high school was in full swing. I had done everything right; I strove to be the best I could be. Excellent grades, good athlete, no drugs, no smoking, no alcohol, good friends, obedient (well, pretty obedient), people pleaser, and I loved my parents.

I was "great" on paper but in my heart and soul something was missing. Whatever was missing was not being satisfied by all that I was doing. Little did I know that it was God, Jesus, and the Holy Spirit pursuing me, nudging me closer to Him.

During my junior year of high school my two best friends Jennifer and Barbie would invite me to their church. I would politely (sometimes not so politely) tell them NO. I told them I had a horrible experience as a child, learning that I didn't need church, nor God! They would always treat me so kindly when accepting my refusals but they wouldn't give up on me. (God didn't give up on me; He used them to pursue me.) Years later, I found out they were continually praying for me that my heart would soften and accept Jesus.

Months went by and they invited me again, but this time it was to a movie that their church was showing.

Mind you this was the '70s and the movie they were showing was "A Thief in the Night." I said, "Yes" just to get them to stop asking! God spoke to me that night and I accepted Him right then and there because I didn't want to go to Hell. I had my "fire insurance." It wasn't a moving experience for me, just a very logical one. God reached me at my level. I loved science and facts, and this seemed that it could happen to me, so I believed. BUT nothing really changed in my heart or behavior. I thought I could do whatever and just not go to Hell because I accepted Jesus. My ticket to Heaven.

I did continue to go to church with Jennifer after Barbie moved away. More seeds were planted, watered, and now were starting to grow.

We both went off to college at Cal State Fullerton and continued to go to church. My heart was softening and my behavior was changing. God was speaking and I was listening.

I am so thankful that Jennifer and Barbie didn't give up on me and for their obedience to God when He asked them to pray for me and be my friend. I will forever be grateful.

Many years have come and gone since the day that Jesus walked through the door of my soul that He had been so patiently waiting for me to open. He brought a joy and fulfillment that cannot be explained except that it's from God and is the foundation of my life.

My life hasn't been free from trials and struggles, but it has also been filled with many blessings from God: a loving husband, two beautiful daughters, loving friends and family, a home, and all that we need.

The cool thing is that I have not had to be on this journey alone. I have God, Jesus, and the Holy Spirit with me. I am not an "only" child anymore; I have brothers and sisters in Christ who make me part of a big family.

I am still growing in Him, far from perfect, and He (Jesus) has taught me to be grateful, loving, kind, and a servant to all I come in contact with.

My life verse is Proverbs 3:5-6, "Trust in the Lord with all your heart and lean not on your own understanding, In all your ways acknowledge Him and He will make your paths straight."

I see now that I was leaning on my own merit (understanding), intelligence, athletic ability, friendships, etc. I thought I didn't need God, but there was that "Jesus-shaped hole" in my soul and heart that could only be filled by Him and nothing else. When that was filled, the striving ceased (for the most part, I am not perfect) and I could turn "Worry into Worship" and "Panic into Praise"!

Does Satan still "haunt" me with thoughts from my past? The answer would be YES but I have the One who is greater than Satan living in me so I have the peace and power to combat it.

So that's it, my story, a simple journey from an only child to a child of God and all that goes with being a part of His family.

Afterword

James 4:13-14, "Now listen, you who say, "Today or tomorrow we will go to this or that city, spend a year there, carry on business and make money. Why, you do not even know what will happen tomorrow. What is your life? You are a mist that appears for a little while and then vanishes."

1 Peter 1:24, "For, 'All people are like grass, and all their glory is like the flowers of the field: the grass withers and the flowers fall.'"

The idea of not knowing when you are going to die hit home with me during an autopsy I was assisting with. A 21-year-old clerk typist died while typing a letter at his desk. The sudden death of this very healthy person presented a mystery that needed an answer. Because of my very skilled mechanical ability and a request from the general in charge of the hospital, I was tasked with brain removal. Upon examination of the brain it was noted that the cerebellum was very deformed. There were hundreds of veins all balled up together. It looked like a ball of spaghetti noodles pointing in a hundred directions all at the same time. I can't recall the exact medical terminology for what this condition is called, but the average lifespan for this malformation is death about two months after being born. This guy should not have made it to 21 years old. But he did. He was a corporal and he'd been in the army more than about two years. And I would guess that he had, like all of us, many dreams and passions that he was looking forward to.

Death has a way of canceling out dreams. One thing death can never take away is your relationship with Jesus. Of course, there is no relationship with Jesus after you die if you did not have one before you die. And die you must if you are a member of Team Human. Don't put off your decision about Jesus. You do not want to go into the second half of life without him.

I have listed an internet contact where you can get more information about Jesus. Also, this website has lots of contacts from around the world with people who have given their lives to Jesus. The internet contact is God-Life.com.

References

Ancient Origins. April 13, 2013, Article, Website.

Bradshaw, Robert I. robibradshaw.com, UK.

Chabad. 2017, The Complete Jewish Bible, with Rashi Commentary, website.

Cliff Notes. 2017, Mythology, Summary and Analysis: Egyptian Mythology The Creation.

Gould, Stephen Jay. 1992, Bully for Brontosaurus: Reflections in Natural History.

Marshall, Michael. New Scientist, July 14, 2009, Timeline: The Evolution of life.

Meeker, Brent. 2017, Cosmology and Cosmogony of Ancient Civilizations.

Ross, Hugh. 1984, The Fingerprint of God.

Ross, Hugh. 2014, Navigating Genesis: A Scientist's Journey through Genesis 1-11.

Smolin, Lee. 2006, The Trouble with Physics: The Rise of String Theory, The Fall of a Science, and What Comes Next.

Made in the USA
San Bernardino, CA
24 February 2020